The Seagull Sartre Library

✳

The Seagull Sartre Library

The Seagull Sartre Library

VOLUME 10

ON BATAILLE
AND BLANCHOT

JEAN-PAUL SARTRE

TRANSLATED BY
CHRIS TURNER

LONDON NEW YORK CALCUTTA

This work is published with the support of
Institut français en Inde – Embassy of France in India

✳

Seagull Books, 2021

Originally published in Jean-Paul Sartre,
Situations I © Éditions Gallimard, Paris, 1947

These essays were first published in English translation
by Seagull Books in *Critical Essays* (2010)
English translation © Christ Turner, 2010

ISBN 978 0 8574 2 913 1

British Library Cataloguing-in-Publication Data
A catalogue record for this book is available
from the British Library

Typeset by Seagull Books, Calcutta, India
Printed and bound in the USA by Integrated Books International

CONTENTS

A NEW MYSTIC

I

There is a crisis of the essay. Elegance and clarity seem to demand that, in this kind of work, we employ a language deader than Latin: the language of Voltaire. I have remarked on this before in relation to *The Myth of Sisyphus*.[1] But if we really try to express today's thoughts using yesterday's language, what a lot of metaphors, circumlocations and imprecise images ensue: you would think we were back in the age of Delille.[2] Some, like Alain[3] and Paulhan,[4] try to be economical with words

---

1 See *Cahiers du Sud* (February 1943).

2 Jacques Delille (1738–1813): a poet renowned for his elaborate circumlocution. [Trans.]

3 Alain was the pen name of the influential French philosopher Emile-Auguste Chartier (1868– 1951). As a teacher at the Lycée Henri IV, Alain counted Simone Weil, Georges Canguilhem and Raymond Aron among his pupils. [Trans.]

4 The reference is to Joë Bousquet, Traduit du Silence (Paris: Gallimard, 1941). [Trans.]

and time, to rein in, by means of numerous ellipses, the florid prolixity that characterizes that language. But how obscure this becomes! Everything is covered with an irritating veneer, whose shimmering surface conceals the ideas. With the American writers, with Kafka and with Camus in France, the contemporary novel has found its style. The style of the essay remains to be discovered. And the style of criticism, too, in my opinion, for I am not unaware, as I write these lines, that I am using an outdated instrument which academic tradition has preserved into our own day.

This is why we must point out a work like that of M. Bataille as deserving of special attention. It is an essay that I would happily describe as agonized (and I have its author's authority to do so, since there are so many mentions of torture and torment in the book). M. Bataille forsakes both the stony speech of the great minds of 1780 and with it, inevitably, the objectivity of the classics. He strips himself bare; he lays himself before us; he isn't pleasant company. If human wretchedness is his theme, then look, he says, at my sores and ulcers. And he opens his clothing to show them to us. Yet lyricism isn't his aim. If he shows himself, he does so in pursuit of proof. Barely has he let us glimpse his wretched nudity and he is covered up again and off we go with him in reasoned discussions of Hegel's system or Descartes's *cogito*. But then the reasoning comes to an abrupt halt and the man reappears. 'I could say,' he writes, for example, in the middle of an argument about God, that 'this hatred is time, but that bothers me. Why should I say time? I feel this hatred when I cry; I analyze nothing.'[5]

Actually, this form which still seems so new, is already part of a tradition. The death of Pascal saved his *Pensées* from being written up into a strong and colourless Apologia. By delivering them to us all jumbled up, by striking down their author before he had the time to muzzle himself, that death made them the model for the genre that concerns us here. And there is, in my view, more than a little of Pascal in M. Bataille, particularly the feverish contempt and the desire to get his words out quickly, to which I shall return. But it is to Nietzsche that he himself refers explicitly. And, indeed certain pages of *Inner Experience*, with their breathless disorder, their passionate symbolism and their tone of prophetic preaching, seem to come straight out of *Ecce Homo* or *The Will to Power*. Lastly, M. Bataille was once very close to the Surrealists and no one cultivated the agonized essay so much as the Surrealists. Breton's voluminous personality found itself at ease in that genre: coldly, in the style of Charles Maurras, he demonstrated the incomparable excellence of his theories, then suddenly went off on to the most puerile details of his life, showing photographs of the restaurants in which he had had lunch and the shop where he bought his coal. There was, in

---

5 Georges Bataille, *Inner Experience* (Albany: State University of New York Press, 1988), p. 102.

that exhibitionism, a need to destroy all literature and, to that end, suddenly to reveal, behind the 'monsters imitated by art', the true monster. There was probably also a taste for scandal, but mainly a preference for direct contact. The book had to establish a kind of fleshly closeness between author and reader. Lastly, in the case of these authors impatient for commitment, who felt contempt for the quiet occupation of writing, every work had to involve risk. As Michel Leiris did in his admirable *Manhood*,[6] they revealed of themselves everything that could shock, annoy or prompt laughter, in order to lend their undertakings the perilous seriousness of a genuine act. Pascal's *Pensées*, Rousseau's *Confessions*, Nietzsche's *Ecce Homo*, *Les Pas Perdus* and *L'Amour Fou* by Breton, *Le Traité du Style* by Aragon and *Manhood*— it is within this series of 'passionate geometries' that Bataille's *Inner Experience* has its place.

Right from the preface, the author informs us that he wants to achieve a synthesis of '*rapture*' and '*rigorous intellectual method*'; that he is trying to make 'rigorous, shared emotional knowledge (laughter)' and 'rational knowledge' coincide.[7] No more is needed for us to see that we are going to find ourselves in the presence of a demonstrative apparatus with a powerful affective potential. But M. Bataille goes further. For him, feeling is both at the origin and at the end: 'Conviction,' he writes,

---

6 Michel Leiris, *Manhood* (London: Jonathan Cape, 1968).

7 Bataille, *Inner Experience*, p. *xxxiii*.

'does not arise from reasoning, but only from the feelings which it defines.'[8] We know these famous ice-cold, yet fiercely blazing lines of reasoning, troubling in their harsh abstraction, that are deployed by the passionate and the paranoid: their rigour is, from the outset, a challenge and a threat; their suspicious immobility harbours forebodings of stormy lava-flows. M. Bataille's syllogisms are like that. They are the proofs supplied by an orator, jealous lover, barrister or madman. Not by a mathematician. We can sense that this plastic, molten substance, with its sudden solidifications that liquify again as soon as we touch them, needs to be rendered in a special form and can never be at home with an all-purpose language. At times, the style is close to choking or drowning in its efforts to render the gasping suffocations of ecstasy or anguish (Pascal's 'Joy, joy, tears of joy' will find a counterpart in such sentences as the following: 'One must. Is this to moan? I no longer know. Where am I going to?' etc. . . .);[9] at others, it is broken up with little bursts of laughter; at yet others, it sprawls out into the balanced periods of reasoning. The sentence of intuitive rapture, condensed into a single instant, is found side by side, in *Inner Experience*, with the leisurely discursive mode.

It is, in fact, only reluctantly that M. Bataille employs this discursive mode. He hates it and, through it, he

---

8 Bataille, *Inner Experience*, p. 18.

9 Bataille, *Inner Experience*, p. 55. It even seems at times that M. Bataille amuses himself by pastiching Pascal's style: 'Should one look at last at the history of men, man by man', etc. (p. 38).

hates all language. M. Bataille shares this hatred—which we also noted recently in Camus—with a great many contemporary writers. But the reasons he gives for it are all his own: it is the mystic's hatred to which he lays claim, not the terrorist's. First, he tells us, language is a project: the speaker has an appointment with himself at the end of the sentence. Speech is a construction, an undertaking; the octogenarian who speaks is as mad as the octogenarian who plants. To speak is to rend oneself apart; to put existence off until later, until the end of the discourse; to be torn between a subject, a verb and a complement. M. Bataille wants to exist fully and immediately—this very instant. Moreover, words are 'the instruments of useful acts': hence, to name the real is to cover it over or veil it with familiarity, to bring it into the ranks of what Hegel termed 'das Bekannte': the *too well known*, which goes unnoticed. To tear away the veils and swap the opaque quietude of knowledge for the astonishment of non-knowledge, a 'holocaust of words' is needed, that holocaust that has already been carried out by poetry:

> Should words such as *horse* or *butter* come into a poem, they do so detached from interested concerns . . . When the farm girl says *butter* or the stable boy says *horse*, they know butter and horses . . . But, *on the contrary, poetry leads from the known to the unknown*. It can do what neither the boy nor the girl can do: introduce a

butter horse. In this way, it sets one before the unknowable.[10]

But poetry doesn't propose to communicate a precise experience. M. Bataille, for his part, has to identify, describe, persuade. Poetry confines itself to sacrificing words; M. Bataille aims to explain to us the reasons for this sacrifice. And it is with words that he must exhort us to sacrifice words. Our author is very conscious of this circle. It is partly for this reason that he situates his work 'beyond poetry'. As a result of this, he becomes subject to a constraint similar to those the tragedians imposed on themselves. Just as Racine could wonder, 'how to express jealousy and fear in rhyming 12-foot lines' and just as he drew his force of expression from that very constraint, so M. Bataille asks himself how he can express silence with words. Perhaps this is a problem that has no philosophical solution; perhaps, from this angle, it is merely a case of wordplay. But from our standpoint, it looks like an aesthetic rule as valid as any other, a supplementary difficulty the author freely imposes on himself, like a billiards player marking out limits for himself on the green baize. It is this difficulty freely consented to that lends the style of *Inner Experience* its particular savour. First, we find in M. Bataille a mimesis of the moment. Silence and the moment being one and the same thing, it is the configuration of the moment he has to impart to his thought. 'The expression of inner experience,' he

---

10 Bataille, *Inner Experience*, pp. 135–6 (translation modified).

writes, 'must in some way respond to its movement.'[11] He therefore eschews the carefully composed work and an ordered development of argument. He expresses himself in short aphorisms, spasms, which the reader can grasp at a single glance and which stand as instantaneous explosions, bounded by two blanks, two abysses of repose. He himself provides the following explanation:

> A continual challenging of everything deprives one of the power of proceeding by separate operations, obliges one to express oneself through rapid flashes, to free as much as is possible the expression of one's thought from a project, to include everything in a few sentences: anguish, decision and the right to the poetic perversion of words without which it would seem that one was subject to a domination.[12]

As a result, the work assumes the appearance of a string of remarks. It is odd to record that the anti-intellectualist Bataille meets up here with the rationalist Alain in his choice of mode of exposition. This is because this 'continual questioning of everything' may just as well proceed from a mystic negation as from a Cartesian philosophy of free judgement. But the resemblance goes no further than this: Alain trusts in words. Bataille, by contrast, will attempt to consign them, in the very weft

---

11 Bataille, *Inner Experience*, p. 6.
12 Bataille, *Inner Experience*, pp. 28–9.

of his text, to the most minor role. They have to be shorn of their ballast, emptied out and imbued with silence, in order to lighten them to the extreme. He will try, then, to use 'slippery sentences', like soapy planks that have us suddenly falling into the ineffable; slippery words too, like this very word 'silence'. He will write of 'the abolition of the sound which the word is; among all words . . . the most perverse and the most poetic.'[13] Alongside those words which signify—words indispensable, after all, to understanding—he will slip into his argument words that are merely suggestive, such as 'laughter', 'torment', 'agony', 'rending', 'poetry', etc., which he diverts from their original meaning to confer on them gradually a magical evocative power. These various techniques lead to a situation in which M. Bataille's deep thought—or feeling—seems entirely encapsulated in each of his 'Reflections'. It doesn't build up, isn't progressively enriched, but rises, undivided and almost ineffable, to the surface of each aphorism, so that each presents the same formidable, complex meaning with a different lighting. By contrast with the analytical methods of the philosophers, we might say that M. Bataille's book presents itself as the product of a totalitarian thinking.

But this thinking itself, syncretic as it may be, could still aim for—and attain to—the universal. M. Camus, for example, no less struck by the absurdity of our condition, has still attempted an objective portrait of 'homo

---

13 Bataille, *Inner Experience*, p. 16.

absurdus', irrespective of historical circumstances, and the great exemplary Absurd individuals to whom he refers—such as Don Juan—have a universality that is every bit the equal of that of Kant's moral agent. Bataille's originality lies in his having, despite his angry, peevish reasoning, deliberately chosen history over metaphysics. Here again, we have to look back to Pascal, whom I would happily call the first *historical* thinker, because he was the first to grasp that, in man, existence precedes essence. There is, in his view, too much grandeur in the human creature for us to understand him on the basis of his wretchedness, too much wretchedness for us to deduce his nature from his grandeur. In a word, something *happened to* man, something undemonstrable and irreducible, and hence something *historical*: fall and redemption. As a historical religion, Christianity stands opposed to all metaphysics. M. Bataille, who was a devout Christian, has retained Christianity's deep sense of historicity. He speaks to us of the human condition, not of human nature: man is not a nature, but a drama; his characteristics are *acts*: project, torment, agony, laughter—so many words referring to temporal processes of realization, not qualities given passively and passively received. This is because M. Bataille's work is, like most mystical writings, the product of a *re-descent*. M. Bataille is returning from an unknown region; he is coming back down among us. He wants to carry us with him: he describes our wretchedness which once was his; he tells us the story of his journey, his long-held delusions, his arrival. If, like the Platonic philosopher brought out from the cave, he had found himself suddenly in the presence of an eternal truth, the historical aspect of his account would probably have been eliminated, giving way to the universal rigour of Ideas. But his encounter was with non-knowledge, and non-knowledge is essentially historical, since it can be described only as a particular experience had by a particular person on a particular date. For this reason, we have to see *Inner Experience* both as a Gospel (though he doesn't impart any 'good news' to us) and an Invitation to the Voyage.[14] Edifying Narrative—that is what he could have called his book. With this—through this mix of proof and drama—the work takes on an entirely original flavour. Alain first wrote his objective *Propos* (Remarks) and only later, as a conclusion to his life's work, his *Histoire de mes Pensées* (History of My Thoughts).[15] But the two are in one here, entangled in the same book. Barely have the proofs been laid before us than they suddenly appear historical: a man thought them, at a certain point in his life, and became a martyr to them. We are reading not just Gide's *The Counterfeiters*, but also 'Édouard's Journal'[16]

14 'Invitation au Voyage' is the title of a famous and much-translated poem in Baudelaire's *Les Fleurs du Mal* [Trans.]

15 Alain wrote a series of 'Propos', including *Propos sur le bonheur* (Paris: Gallimard, 1925), *Propos de politique* (Paris: Éditions Rieder, 1934) and *Propos de littérature* (Paris: Paul Hartmann, 1934); his *Histoire de mes pensées* was published by Gallimard in 1936. [Trans.]

16 This journal maintains the purported narrator's running commentary within the novel on André Gide's *Les Faux-Monnayeurs* (1925). [Trans.]

and *The Journal of the Counterfeiters*.[17] In conclusion, the subjectivity closes over both the reasoning and the rapture. It is a man that stands before us, a man naked and alone, who disarms all his deductions by dating them, a man both unlikable and 'captivating'—like Pascal.

Have I conveyed the originality of this language? One last feature will help me to do so: the tone is constantly scornful. It recalls the disdainful aggressiveness of the Surrealists; M. Bataille wants to rub his readers up the wrong way. Yet, he writes to 'communicate'. But it seems that he speaks to us reluctantly. And is he actually addressing us? Indeed he is not—and he is at pains to let us know. He 'loathes his own voice'. Though he regards communication as necessary—for ecstasy without communication is mere emptiness—he says: 'I become irritated when I think of the time of 'activity' which I spent—during the last years of peacetime—in forcing myself to reach my fellow beings.'[18] And we must take this term 'fellow beings' in its strictest sense. It is for the mystic's apprentice that M. Bataille writes, for the person who, in solitude, is making his way, through laughter and world-weariness, towards his final torment. But there is nothing comforting for our author in the hope that he will be read by this very particular sort of

---

17 The latter journal, published separately in 1927, was (or at least claims to be) Gide's journal at the time of writing *Les Faux-Monnayeurs*. [Trans.]

18 Bataille, *Inner Experience*, p. 92.

Nathanaël.[19] 'Even in preaching to the converted, there is, in its predication, a distressful element.'[20] Even if we were this potential disciple, we have the right to listen to M. Bataille, but not—he loftily warns us—to judge him: 'There are no readers, nevertheless, who have in them anything to cause . . . [my] disarray. Were the most perspicacious of them to accuse me, I would laugh: it is of myself that I am afraid.'[21] This puts the critic at his ease. M. Bataille opens up here, strips himself bare before our very eyes, but at the same time he curtly rejects our judgement: it is for him alone to judge and the communication he wishes to establish is without reciprocity. He is on high, we are down below. He delivers us a message and it is for us to receive it if we can. But what adds to our difficulty is that the summit from which he speaks to us is at the same time the 'abyssal' depth of abjection.

The proud and dramatic preaching of a man more than halfway committed to silence, who, to go as quickly as he can, reluctantly speaks a feverish, bitter and often incorrect language and who exhorts us, without looking at us directly, to join him proudly in his shame and darkness—this is what *Inner Experience* seems at first to

---

19 Nathanaël is the disciple to whom André Gide's *Les nourritures terrestres* (1928) is addressed. [Trans.]

20 Bataille, *Inner Experience*, p. 92. The original French here is: '*Même à prêcher des convaincus, il est dans la prédication un élément de détresse.*' It seems odd to read '*prédication*' here in the grammatical sense of 'predication', rather than to take it to refer to its everyday meaning of 'preaching'. [Trans.]

21 Bataille, *Inner Experience*, p. 66.

be. Apart from a little empty bombast and some clumsiness in the handling of abstractions, everything in this mode of expression is praiseworthy: it presents the essayist with an example and a tradition; it takes us back to the sources, to Pascal and Montaigne, and at the same time it offers us a language and a syntax better adapted to the problems of our age. But form isn't everything. Let us look at the content.

II

There are people you might call survivors. Early on, they lost a beloved person—father, friend or mistress—and their lives are merely the gloomy aftermath of that death. Monsieur Bataille is a survivor of the death of God. And, when one thinks about it, it would seem that our entire age is surviving that death, which he experienced, suffered and survived. God is dead. We should not understand by that that He does not exist, nor even that He now no longer exists. He is dead: he used to speak to us and he has fallen silent, we now touch only his corpse. Perhaps he has slipped out of the world to some other place, like a dead man's soul. Perhaps all this was merely a dream. Hegel tried to replace Him with his system and the system has collapsed. Comte tried with the religion of humanity, and positivism has collapsed. In France and elsewhere, around the year 1880, a number of honourable Gentlemen, some of them sufficiently logical to demand they be cremated after their deaths, had the notion of developing a secular morality. We lived by that morality for a time, but then along came M. Bataille—and so many others like him—to attest to its bankruptcy. God is dead, but man has not, for all that, become atheistic. Today, as yesterday, this silence of the transcendent, combined with modern man's enduring religious need, is the great question of the age. It is the problem that torments Nietzsche, Heidegger and Jaspers. It is our author's central personal drama. Coming out of a 'long Christian piety', his life 'dissolved into laughter'. Laughter was a revelation:

> Fifteen years ago . . . I was returning from I don't know where, late at night . . . Crossing the rue du Four, I suddenly became unknown to myself in this 'nothingness' . . . I denied the grey walls that enclosed me, I plunged into a kind of rapture. I was laughing divinely: the umbrella that had come down over my head covered me (I deliberately covered myself with this black shroud). I was laughing as no one perhaps had laughed before; the bottom of every thing lay open, was laid bare, as though I were dead.[22]

For some time, he attempted to sidestep the consequences of these revelations. Eroticism, the all-too-human 'sacred' of sociology, offered him some precarious havens. And then everything collapsed and here he is

---

22 Bataille, *Inner Experience*, p. 34 (translation modified).

before us, lugubrious and comical, like an inconsolable widower indulging, all dressed in black, in 'the solitary vice' in memory of his dead wife. For M. Bataille refuses to reconcile these two immovable and contradictory demands: God is silent, I cannot budge an inch on that; everything in me calls out for God, I cannot forget Him. At more than one point in *Inner Experience*, you would think you had Stravogin or Ivan Karamazov before you—an Ivan who had known André Breton. From this there arises, in Bataille's case, a particular experience of the absurd. In fact, that experience is found in one form or another in most contemporary authors. One thinks of the 'fissure' in Jaspers, death in Malraux, Heidegger's 'abandonment', Kafka's temporarily reprieved creatures, the pointless, obsessive labour of Sisyphus in Camus, or Blanchot's Aminadab.

But it must be said that modern thought has encountered two kinds of absurd. For some, the fundamental absurdity is 'facticity' or, in other words, the irreducible contingency of our 'being-there', of our existence that has neither purpose nor reason. For others, faithless disciples of Hegel, it resides in the fact that man is an insoluble contradiction. It is this absurdity M. Bataille feels most sharply. Like Hegel, whom he has read, he takes the view that reality is conflict. But, for him, as for Kierkegaard, Nietzsche and Jaspers, there are conflicts that have no resolution. He eliminates the moment of synthesis from the Hegelian trinity, and, for the dialectical view of the world, he substitutes a tragic—or, as he would put it, dramatic—vision. The reader will perhaps be put in mind of Camus here, whose fine novel we commented on recently. But for Camus, who has barely dipped into the phenomenologists and whose thinking falls within the tradition of the French moralists, the original contradiction is a matter of fact. There are forces in presence—which are what they are—and the absurdity arises out of the relation between them. The contradiction comes retrospectively. For M. Bataille, who is more intimately familiar with existentialism and has even borrowed his terminology from it, the absurd is not given, but *produces itself.* Man creates himself as conflict. We are not made of a certain stuff in which fissures might appear through wear and tear or the action of some external agent. The 'fissure'[23] fissures only itself; it is its own substance and man is the unity of that substance: a strange unity that inspires nothing at all, but, rather, destroys itself to maintain the opposition. Kierkegaard called this ambiguity: in it contradictions co-exist without merging; each one leads on indefinitely to another. It is this perpetual evanescent unity that M. Bataille experiences immediately within himself; it is this which provides him with his original vision of the absurd and the image he constantly employs to express that vision: the image of a self-opening wound whose swollen lips gape open towards the heavens. Should we

---

23 This '*déchirure*' or 'fissure' is found in Jaspers and in M. Bataille. Is this evidence of influence? M. Bataille doesn't quote Jaspers, but he seems to have read him.

then, you will ask, place M. Bataille among the existentialist thinkers? That would be too hasty. M. Bataille
doesn't like philosophy. His aim is to relate a certain
experience to us or, rather, we should say, a certain *lived
experience*, in the sense of the German word *Erlebnis*.[24]
It is a question of life and death, pain and delight, not
tranquil contemplation. (M. Bataille's mistake is to
believe that modern philosophy has remained contem-
plative. He has clearly not understood Heidegger, of
whom he speaks often and ineptly). As a result, if he does
use philosophical techniques, he does so as a more convenient way of expressing an adventure that lies beyond
philosophy, on the borders of knowledge and non-
knowledge. But philosophy takes its revenge: this technical material, employed without discernment, bowled
along by polemical or dramatic passion and dragooned
into rendering the pantings and spasms of our author,
turns round against him. When inserted in M. Bataille's
texts, words that had precise meanings in the works of
Hegel or Heidegger lend it a semblance of rigorous
thought. But as soon as you attempt to grasp that
thought, it melts like snow. The emotion alone remains,
that is to say, a powerful inner disturbance in respect of
vague objects. 'Of poetry, I will now say that it is . . . the
sacrifice in which words are victims,' writes M. Bataille.[25]

---

24 It is, in fact, only in the German language, as *Das innere Erlebnis*,
that the book's title will have its full meaning. The French word
'expérience' misrepresents our author's intentions.

25 Bataille, *Inner Experience*, p. 135.

In this sense, his work is a burnt offering of philosophical words. As soon as he uses one, its meaning immediately curdles or goes off like warm milk. Moreover, in his haste to *bear witness*, M. Bataille regales us with thoughts from very different dates in no particular order, but he doesn't tell us whether we are to regard them as the paths that have led him to his current state of feeling or as ways of seeing that he still holds to today. From time to time, he seems in the grip of a feverish desire to unify them; at other times, he relaxes, abandons them and they go back to their isolation. If we attempt to organize this vague assemblage, we must first remind ourselves that each word is a trap and that he is trying to trick us by presenting as thoughts the violent stirrings of a soul in mourning. Furthermore, M. Bataille, who is neither a scholar nor a philosopher, has, unfortunately, a smattering of science and philosophy. We run up straight away against two distinct attitudes of mind that coexist within him, without his realizing it, and that are mutually detrimental: the existentialist attitude and what I shall dub, for want of a better word, the scientistic. As we know, it was scientism that scrambled Nietzsche's message, deflecting him into childish views on evolution and masking his understanding of the human condition. It is scientism too that will distort the whole of M. Bataille's thought.

The starting point is that man is born from— 'is begotten of'—the earth: We may take this to mean that he is the product of one of the countless possible combinations of natural elements. A highly improbable combination, we guess, as improbable as cubes with letters on them rolling on the ground arranging themselves in such a way as to spell out the word 'anticonstitutional'. 'A single chance decided the possibility of this *self* which I am: in the end the mad improbability of the sole being without whom, *for me*, nothing would be, becomes evident.'[26] There you have a scientistic, objective viewpoint if ever there was one. And, indeed, in order to adopt it, we have to assert the anteriority of the object (Nature) over the subject; we must, from the outset, place ourselves outside of inner experience—the only experience available to us. We have to accept the value of science as a basic assumption. And yet science doesn't tell us that we came from the earth: it simply tells us about earth. M. Bataille is scientistic in the sense that he makes science say much more than it really does. We are, then, it seems, poles apart from an *Erlebnis* on the part of the subject, from a concrete encounter of existence with itself: at the moment of the *cogito*, Descartes never saw himself as a product of Nature; he registered his own contingency and facticity, the irrationality of his 'being-there', not his improbability. But here everything changes suddenly: this 'improbability'—which can be deduced only from the calculation of the *chances* of the play of natural forces producing just *this*, this *Self*—is presented to us as the original content of the *cogito*. 'The feeling of my fundamental improbability situates me in

26 Bataille, *Inner Experience*, p. 69.

the world,' writes M. Bataille.[27] And, a little further on, he rejects the reassuring constructs of reason in the name of the 'experience of the self, of its improbability, of its insane demands'.[28] How can he not see that improbability is not an immediate given, but precisely a construct of the reason? It is the *Other* who is improbable, because I apprehend him from outside. But, in an initial conceptual slide, our author equates facticity, the concrete object of an authentic experience, with improbability, a pure scientific concept. Looking further, we find that, according to Bataille, this feeling brings us into contact with our deepest being. What a mistake! Improbability can only be a hypothesis that is closely dependent on earlier presuppositions. I am improbable if a certain universe is assumed to be true. If God created me, if I was subject to a particular decree of Providence or if I am a mode of Spinozist substance, my improbability disappears. Our author's starting point is, then, *something deduced*; it is in no way encountered by feeling. But we shall see another piece of trickery: M. Bataille goes on to equate improbability with irreplaceability: 'I,' he writes, 'that is to say, the infinite, painful improbability of an irreplaceable being, which I am.'[29] And this identification is even clearer a few lines later:

> The empirical knowledge of my similarity with others is irrelevant, for the essence of my self

---

27 Bataille, *Inner Experience*, p. 69.

28 Bataille, *Inner Experience*, p. 70.

29 Bataille, *Inner Experience*, p. 69.

arises from this—that nothing will be able to replace it: the feeling of my fundamental improbability situates me in the world where I remain as though foreign to it, absolutely foreign.[30]

In this same way, Gide didn't need to advise Nathanaël to *become* the most irreplaceable of human beings: irreplaceability, which makes every person a Unique Entity, is given from the outset. It is a quality we are endowed with, since what is *unique* in me is, in the end, the '*single* chance' that 'decided the possibility of this self'.[31] Thus, in conclusion, this self is not me: it eludes me; it no more belongs to me than the movement belongs to the billiard ball. It was imparted to me from the outside. M. Bataille calls this external idiosyncracy 'ipseity' and the very name he gives to it reveals his perpetual confusion with regard to scientism and existentialism. The word 'ipseity' is a neologism he takes from Corbin, Heidegger's translator. M. Corbin uses it to render the German term *Selbstheit*, which means existential return towards oneself on the basis of the project. It is from this return to oneself that the *self* emerges. Hence, ipseity is a reflexive relationship that one creates by living it out. Once in possession of the word, M. Bataille applies it to knives, machines and even attempts to apply

---

30 Bataille, *Inner Experience*, p. 69.

31 'Linked to the birth then to the union of a man and a woman, and even, at the moment of their union . . .' (Bataille, *Inner Experience*, p. 69).

it to the atom (then thinks better of it). This is because he understands it merely to mean *natural individuality*. The rest follows automatically: noticing its 'ipseity', the product of the 'most madly improbable chance', the self sets itself up defiantly above the void of Nature. We come back here to the inner attitude of existentialism: 'Human bodies are erect on the ground like a challenge to the Earth . . .'[32] Improbability has been internalized; it has become a fundamental, lived, accepted, claimed experience. This brings us back to the 'challenge' that lies, for Jaspers, at the beginning of all history. The self demands its ipseity; it wishes to 'climb to the pinnacle'. And M. Bataille tops Jaspers off with Heidegger: the authentic experience of my improbable ipseity is not given to me ordinarily, he tells us.

> As long as I live, I am content with a coming and going, with a compromise. No matter what I say, I know myself to be a member of a species and I remain in harmony, roughly speaking, with a common reality; I take part in what, by all necessity, exists—in what nothing can withdraw. The Self-that-dies abandons this harmony: it truly perceives what surrounds it to be a void and itself to be a challenge to this void.[33]

---

32 Bataille, *Inner Experience*, p. 78 (translation modified).

33 Bataille, *Inner Experience*, p. 71.

This is the meaning of human reality in the light of its 'being-for-death'. Just as Heidegger speaks of a freedom that launches itself against death (*Freiheit zum Tod*), so M. Bataille writes: 'the *self* grows until it reaches the pure imperative: this imperative . . . is formulated "die like a dog".'[34] Isn't this irreplaceability of 'human reality', experienced in the blinding light of being-for-death, precisely the Heideggerian experience? Yes, but M. Bataille doesn't stop at that: the fact is that this experience, which ought to be pure, *suffered* apperception of the self by itself, bears within it a seed of destruction; in Heidegger we discover only the *inside* and we are nothing except insofar as we discover ourselves; being coincides with the movement of discovery. For his part, M. Bataille has poisoned his experience, since he actually makes it bear upon improbability, a hypothetical concept borrowed from external reality. In this way, the outside has slipped inside myself; death illumines only a fragment of Nature; at the point where the urgency of death reveals me to myself, M. Bataille has silently arranged that I should see myself through the eyes of another. The consequence of this piece of legerdemain is that 'Death is in a sense an imposture.' Since the Self is an external object, it has the 'exteriority' of natural things.[35] This means, first of all, that it is *composite* and that the grounds of its compositeness lie outside itself: 'A being

---

34 Bataille, *Inner Experience*, p. 72.

35 In the sense in which Hegel tells us, 'Nature is externality.'

is always a set of particles whose relative autonomies are maintained'[36] and 'This being *ipse*, itself constituted from parts and, as such—being result, unpredictable chance—enters the universe as the will for autonomy.'[37] These remarks are made, once again, from the scientific standpoint: it is science which, by its desire for analysis, dissolves individualities and relegates them to the realm of appearances. And it is the scientist again who, looking at human life *from the outside*, can write:

> What you are stems from the activity which links the innumerable elements which constitute you to the intense communication of these elements among themselves. These are contagions of energy, of movement, of warmth, or transfers of elements, which constitute inevitably the life of your organized being. Life is never situated at a particular point; it passes rapidly from one point to another (or from multiple points to other points), like a current or like a sort of streaming of electricity. Thus, where you would like to grasp your timeless substance, you encounter only a slipping, only the poorly coordinated play of your perishable elements.[38]

36 Bataille, *Inner Experience*, p. 85 (translation modified).

37 Bataille, *Inner Experience*, p. 74 (translation modified).

38 Bataille, *Inner Experience*, p. 94 (translation modified).

Moreover, ipseity is subject to the solvent action of time. M. Bataille takes over Proust's remarks on time as separator. He doesn't see the balancing element: namely, that *durée* also—and primarily—fulfils a binding role. Time, he says, 'signifies only the flight of the objects that seemed true'[39] and, he adds, 'as is the case with time, the self-that-dies is pure change, and neither one nor the other have real existence.'[40]

What, then, but scientific time is this time that gnaws away and separates—this time each instant of which corresponds to a position of a moving object on a trajectory? Is M. Bataille sure that a genuine *inner* experience of time would have yielded the same results? The fact remains that, for him, this 'reprieved' self that is never finished, made up of components external to one another is—though it reveals itself to the dying subject—merely a sham. We see the emergence of the tragic here: we are an appearance striving to be a reality, but whose very efforts to leave its phantom existence behind are mere semblance. We can, however, also see the *explanation* for this sense of the tragic: the fact is that M. Bataille adopts two contradictory viewpoints simultaneously. On the one hand, he seeks—and finds— himself by a procedure analogous to the *cogito*, which reveals to him his irreplaceable individuality; on the other hand, he suddenly steps outside himself to examine that

---

39 Bataille, *Inner Experience*, p. 74 (translation modified).
40 Bataille, *Inner Experience*, p. 74.

individuality with the eyes and instruments of the scientist, as though it were a thing in the world. And this latter point of view assumes that he has taken on board a certain number of postulates on the value of science and analysis and on the nature of objectivity, postulates he would have to sweep away if he wanted immediate access to himself. As a result, the object of his enquiry seems a strange, contradictory entity, very similar to Kierkegaard's 'ambiguous creatures': it is a reality that is, nonetheless, illusory, a unity that crumbles into multiplicity, a cohesion that time tears apart. But these contradictions are not to be wondered at: if M. Bataille found them in himself, that is because he put them there, forcibly introducing the transcendent into the immanent. If he had kept to the viewpoint of inner discovery, he would have understood: (1) that the data of science have no part in the certainty of the *cogito* and that they have to be regarded as merely probable; if one confines oneself to one's inner experience, one cannot come out again to observe oneself from the outside; (2) that in the field of inner experience, there no longer are any appearances; or, rather, that, in that experience, appearance is absolute reality. If I dream of a perfume, it is not a real perfume. But if I dream that I take pleasure in smelling it, then that is *true* pleasure; you cannot dream your pleasure, you cannot dream the simplicity or unity of your *Self*. If you discover them, then they exist, because you give them existence by discovering them; (3) that there is nothing troubling about the famous temporal rending of the Self. For time also binds and the Self in its very being is temporal. This means that, far from being nullified by Time, it has need of Time to realize itself. And I shall have nothing of the objection that the Self fades away by fragments, by moments, for the Time of inner experience is not made up of moments.

But M. Bataille is at the second stage of the analysis now, the stage that will reveal to us the permanent contradiction that we *are*. The *ipse*, the unstable unity of particles, is itself a particle in larger entities. This is what M. Bataille calls *communication*. He notes quite rightly that the relations established between human beings cannot be limited to mere relations of juxtaposition. Human beings do not first exist and then communicate afterwards; communication constitutes them in their being from the outset. Here again, we might at first believe we are in the presence of the latest philosophical advances of Phenomenology. Isn't this 'communication' reminiscent of Heidegger's *Mitsein*? But, as before, this existential resonance appears illusory as soon as we look more closely. 'A man,' writes M. Bataille, 'is a particle inserted in unstable and tangled groups,'[41] and elsewhere,

> Knowledge which the male neighbour has of his female neighbour is no less removed from an encounter of strangers than is life from death. *Knowledge* appears in this way like an unstable

---

41 Bataille, *Inner Experience*, p. 84.

biological bond—no less real, however, than that of cells of a tissue. The exchange between two persons possesses in effect the power to survive momentary separation.[42]

He adds that 'Only the instability of the relations . . . permits the illusion of a being which is isolated . . .' In this way, the *ipse* is doubly illusory: illusory because it is composite and illusory because it is a component. M. Bataille brings out the two complementary and opposing aspects of any organized ensemble: 'constitution transcending the constituent parts, relative autonomy of the constituent parts'.[43] This is a good description: it is akin to Meyerson's insights into what he termed 'the fibrous structure of the universe'. But he was, precisely, describing the universe or, in other words, Nature outside the subject. To apply these principles to the community of subjects is to reinsert them into Nature. How, in fact, can M. Bataille apprehend this 'constitution transcending the constituent parts'? It can only be by observing his own existence, since he is merely an element within an ensemble. The floating unity of the elements can be evident only to an observer who has deliberately placed himself outside this totality. But only God is outside. And even then, we would have to be speaking of a God that is different from Spinoza's. Moreover, the discovery of a reality that is not *our* reality can

---

42 Bataille, *Inner Experience*, p. 84.

43 Bataille, *Inner Experience*, p. 85.

be made only through a hypothesis and its status is never anything more than probable. How are we to align the inner certainty of our existence with this probability that it may belong to these unstable ensembles? And, logically, shouldn't the subordination of the terms be reversed: isn't it our autonomy that becomes certainty and our dependency that is consigned to the realm of illusion? For if I am the consciousness *of* my dependency, then dependency is an object and consciousness is independent. Moreover, the law M. Bataille establishes isn't limited to the field of human interrelations. In the texts we have cited, he extends it expressly to the entire organized universe. If it applies, then, to living cells as much as to subjects, this can only be insofar as subjects are regarded as cells or, in other words, as things. And the law is no longer the simple description of an inner experience, but an abstract principle, akin to those that govern mechanics and, at the same time, several regions of the universe. If it were sentient, the falling stone wouldn't discover the law of gravity in its own fall. It would experience its fall as a unique event. The law of gravity would, for that stone, be a law applying to *other stones*.

Similarly, when he legislates on 'communication', M. Bataille is necessarily speaking of the communication of the Others among themselves. We recognize this attitude: the subject establishes a law by induction from the empirical observation of other human beings, then employs analogical reasoning to place himself under the sway of the law he has just established. This is the attitude of the sociologist. Not for nothing was M. Bataille a member of that strange and famous Collège de Sociologie that would have so surprised the honest Durkheim, whom it claimed, among others, as its inspiration and each member of which was using an emergent science to pursue extra-scientific designs. In the Collège M. Bataille learned to treat human beings as things. These volatile, incomplete totalities that suddenly form and become entangled, only to decompose immediately and reform elsewhere, are more akin to the 'unanimist lives' of Romains[44] and, above all, to the 'collective consciousnesses' of the French sociologists than to Heideggerian *Mitsein*.

Was it by chance that these sociologists—Durkheim,[45] Lévy-Bruhl[46] and Bouglé[47]—were the ones, towards the end of the last century, who vainly attempted to lay the foundations of a secular morality? Is it any accident that M. Bataille, the bitterest witness to their failure, has taken over their vision of the social, transcended it

44 Jules Romains (1885–1972): a French novelist and the founder of the Unanimist literary movement. [Trans.]

45 Émile Durkheim (1858–1917): one of the founding fathers of modern sociology. [Trans.]

46 Lucien Lévy-Bruhl (1857–1939): a sociologist and ethnologist with a strong interest in what was known in his day as 'the primitive mind'. [Trans.]

47 Célestin Bouglé (1870–1940): a philosopher who turned to the social sciences and became, alongside Durkheim, one of the first editors of *L'Année Sociologique*. [Trans.]

and stolen the notion of the 'sacred' from them, in order to adapt it for his personal ends? But the point is that the sociologist cannot integrate himself into sociology: he remains the one creating it. He cannot be part of it, any more than Hegel can be part of Hegelianism or Spinoza of Spinozism. In vain does M. Bataille attempt to enter into the machinery he has set up: he remains outside, with Durkheim and Hegel and God the Father. We shall see, shortly, that he surreptitiously sought out that privileged position.

However this may be, we have now pinned down the contradiction: the self is autonomous and dependent. When it considers its autonomy, it wants to be *ipse*: 'I want to carry my person to the pinnacle,' writes our author.[48] When it experiences its dependence, it wants *to be everything*, that is to say, it wants to expand to the point where it embraces within itself the totality of the constituent parts:

> The uncertain opposition of autonomy to transcendence puts being into a position which slips: each being *ipse*—at the same time that it encloses itself in autonomy, and for this very reason—wants to become the whole of transcendence: in the first place, the whole of the constitution of which it is a part, then one day, without limits, the whole of the universe.[49]

---

48 Bataille, *Inner Experience*, p. 66.
49 Bataille, *Inner Experience*, p. 85 (translation modified).

The contradiction becomes glaringly obvious: it lies both in the situation of the subject that is split in this way between two opposing exigencies and in the very end it wishes to attain:

> The universal God . . . is alone at the summit, even allows himself to be taken for the totality of things and can only arbitrarily maintain "ipseity" within himself. In their history, men are thus engaged in the strange battle of *ipse*, which must become everything and can only become it by dying.[50]

I shall not, with M. Bataille, go over the ins and outs of this vain struggle—this battle that is lost before it begins. At times man wishes to be everything (the desire for power, for absolute knowledge), at times 'the individual, lost in the multitude, delegates to those who occupy its centre the concern for taking on the totality of "being". He is content to "take part" in total existence, which maintains, even in simple cases, a diffuse character.'[51]

Our existence is, in any event, 'an exasperated attempt to complete being'.[52] The horror of our condition is such that most of the time we give up and attempt to escape from ourselves into the *project* or, in other words, into those thousand little activities that have a

---

50 Bataille, *Inner Experience*, pp. 87–8.

51 Bataille, *Inner Experience*, p. 87.

52 Bataille, *Inner Experience*, p. 89.

merely limited meaning and that mask the contradiction by the purposes they project forward. But in vain:

> Man cannot, by any means, escape insufficiency, nor renounce ambition. His will to flee is the fear which he has of being man: its only effect is hypocrisy—the fact that man is what he is without daring to be so . . . There is no concurrence imaginable, and man, inevitably, must wish to be everything, remain *ipse*.[53]

'Project' here is another existentialist's word. It is the received translation of a Heideggerian term. And, as a result, M. Bataille, who undoubtedly borrowed the word from Corbin, seems at times to conceive the project as a fundamental structure of human reality—as when he writes, for example, that 'the world . . . of project is the world in which we find ourselves. War disturbs it, it is true: the world of project remains, but in doubt and anguish,' and we 'emerge through project from the realm of project'.[54] But even though there still seems to be some vacillation in our author's thinking here, a rapid examination is enough to set us right: the project is only a particular form of flight: if it is essential, it is so only to the modern Westerner. The equivalent is not so much to be sought in Heidegger's philosophy as in Kierkegaard's 'ethical man'. And the opposition between project and

---

53 Bataille, *Inner Experience*, p. 91.
54 Bataille, *Inner Experience*, p. 46.

'torment' strangely resembles the opposition Kierkegaard establishes between the moral and the religious life. In fact the project pertains to the concern to compose one's life. The man who makes projects thinks of the morrow and the day after that. He sketches out the plan of his entire life and sacrifices each detail—that is to say, each moment—to the order of the whole. This is what Kierkegaard symbolized in the example of the married man, the head of the family. This perpetual sacrificing of immediate life to the laid-out, fissured life of discourse, M. Bataille likens to the *esprit de sérieux*: project is 'the serious side of existence'.[55] A wretched seriousness that *takes* time, that throws itself into time: 'It is a paradoxical way of being in time: *it is the putting off of existence to a later point*.'[56] But he is more scornful of the serious man than Kierkegaard was of the ethical: this is because seriousness is a *fuite en avant*. M. Bataille is reminiscent of Pascal when he writes: 'One has egotistical satisfaction only in projects . . . one falls in this way into flight, like an animal into an endless trap; on one day or another, one dies an idiot.'[57] The fact is that the project is, in the end, identical with Pascal's *divertissement*; our author would happily condemn the man of projects for 'being unable to sit still in a room'. Behind our agitation, he uncovers—and wishes to get back to—an atrocious

55 Bataille, *Inner Experience*, p. 48.

56 Bataille, *Inner Experience*, p. 46 (translation amended).

57 Bataille, *Inner Experience*, p. 49.

stillness. We shall speak of this in a moment. What we must note at this point is that, in his horror of the temporal fissure, M. Bataille has affinities with an entire family of thinkers who, whether mystical or sensual, rationalistic or otherwise, envisaged time as a separating, negating power and believed that man won himself from time by cleaving to himself in the moment. For these thinkers—Descartes must be ranked among them, as must Epicurus, Rousseau and Gide—discourse, planning, utilitarian memory, *la raison raisonnante* and enterprise wrest us from ourselves. Against this they oppose the moment—the intuitive moment of Cartesian reason, the ecstatic moment of mysticism, the anguished, eternal instant of Kierkegaardian freedom, the moment of Gidean enjoyment, the instant of Proustian remembrance. What unites thinkers who are otherwise so different is the desire to exist right now and to the full. In the *cogito* Descartes believes he grasps himself in his totality as 'res cogitans'; similarly, 'Gidean purity' is the entire possession of oneself and the world in the enjoyment and plundering of the instant. This is the ambition of our author too: he too wishes to 'exist without delay'. His project is to exit from the world of projects.

It is laughter that will enable him to do this. Not that the man-in-project, so long as he continues to battle, is comical: 'everything remains suspended within him.' But a new vista can open up: with a failure or setback, suddenly laughter peals out, just as, for Heidegger, the world suddenly begins to glow with the prospect of machines getting out of kilter, tools being broken. We recognize this laughter of Bataille's: it isn't the plain, inoffensive laughter of Bergson. It is a forced laughter. It has its forerunners: it was through humour that Kierkegaard escaped the ethical life; it was irony that was to liberate Jaspers. But there is, above all, the laughter of Nietzsche: it is that laughter, first and foremost, that M. Bataille wants to make his own. And he quotes this note penned by the author of *Zarathustra*: 'To see tragic natures sink and to be able to laugh at them, despite the profound understanding, the emotion and the sympathy which one feels—that is divine.'[58] However, Nietzsche's laughter is lighter: he terms it 'exuberance' and Zarathustra likens it explicitly to dance. M. Bataille's laughter is bitter and studied; it may be that M. Bataille laughs a lot when he is alone, but nothing of it passes into his work. He tells us that he laughs, but he doesn't make us laugh. He would like to be able to write of his work what Nietzsche writes of *The Gaya Scienza*: 'in practically every sentence of this book profundity and exuberance go hand in hand.'[59] Yet the reader cries out here: profundity maybe, but exuberance!

Laughter is 'a *communal* and *disciplined* emotional knowledge'.[60] The laughing subject is 'the unanimous crowd'. By that, M. Bataille seems to accept that what is

58 Bataille, *Inner Experience*, p. *xxxi*.

59 Friedrich Nietzsche, *Ecce homo. How One Becomes What One Is* (R. J. Hollingdale trans.) (London: Penguin, 1979), p. 98.

60 Bataille, *Inner Experience*, p. *xxxiii*.

described is a collective phenomenon. Yet there he is, laughing alone. No matter: this belongs, no doubt, among those countless contradictions we shall not even attempt to point up. But *of what* is there knowledge here? This, our author tells us, is 'the puzzle . . . which, solved, would itself solve everything.'[61] That certainly pricks our curiosity. But what disappointment a little later on when we get the solution: man is characterized by his desire for sufficiency and laughter is caused by the sense of an insufficiency. More precisely, it *is* the sense of insufficiency.

> If I pull the rug out from under . . . the sufficiency of a solemn figure is followed suddenly by the revelation of an ultimate insufficiency.[62] I am made happy, no matter what, by failure experienced. And I myself lose my seriousness as I laugh. As if it were a relief to escape the concern for my sufficiency.[63]

Is this everything? So *all forms* of laughter are revelations of insufficiency? *All encounters with insufficiency* express themselves through laughter? I can hardly believe this: I could cite a thousand individual cases . . . But I am not criticizing at this point, just laying out the argument. It is merely to be regretted that M. Bataille's 'ideas'

---

61 Bataille, *Inner Experience*, p. 66.

62 Here again, a German word would render M. Bataille's thought better, the word being *Unselbstständigkeit*.

63 Bataille, *Inner Experience*, p. 89 (translation modified).

should be so formless and flabby when his feeling is so firm. To summarize, laughter now grows up: at first it has children and fools as its butt, whom it throws off towards the periphery, but in a reversal it turns back on the father, the leader and all those charged with ensuring the permanence of social combinations and symbolizing the sufficiency of all that the *ipse* wishes to be:

> If I now compare the constitution of society to a pyramid, it appears as domination by the summit . . . The summit incessantly consigns the foundation to insignificance and, in this sense, waves of laughter traverse the pyramid, contesting step by step the pretence of self-importance of the beings placed at a lower level. But the first pattern of these waves issued from the summit ebbs and the second pattern traverses the pyramid from bottom to top: in this instance the backwash contests the self-importance of the beings placed at a higher level . . . it cannot fail . . . to strike at [the summit] . . . And if it strikes at it, what ensues are the death throes of God in darkest night.[64]

A strong image, but loose thinking.[65] We are familiar with this wave that rises to the rafters and leaves only

---

64 Bataille, *Inner Experience*, p. 90 (translation modified).

65 A conception akin to the Surrealists' notion of 'black humour', which is also radical destruction.

scattered stones in the shadows. But there is no other reason to call it laughter than M. Bataille's arbitrary decision to do so. It is also the critical spirit, analysis, dark revolt. It may even be noted that revolutionaries, who are the most convinced of the insufficiency of the commanding heights, are the most serious people in the world. Satire and pamphleteering come from on high. Conservatives excel at it; by contrast, it took years of labour to build up a semblance of revolutionary humour. And even then it looked less a direct insight into the ridiculous and more a painful translation of serious considerations.

However this may be, M. Bataille's laughter is not an inner experience. For himself, the *ipse* seeking 'to become everything' is 'tragic'. But, by revealing the insufficiency of the total edifice in which we believed we occupied a reassuring, comfortable place, laughter, at its height, plunges us suddenly into horror: not the slightest veil subsists between ourselves and the dark night of our insufficiency. We are not everything; no one is everything; being is nowhere. Thus, just as Plato accompanies his dialectical movement with the *askesis* of love, we might speak in M. Bataille's thinking of a kind of *askesis* through laughter. But laughter here is *the negative* in the Hegelian sense. 'At first I had laughed, upon emerging from a long Christian piety, my life having dissolved, with a spring-like bad faith, in laughter.'[66] This negative dissolution that wanders off into all the Surrealist forms

---

66 Bataille, *Inner Experience*, p. 66.

of disrespect and sacrilege, must, by dint of the fact that it is experienced, have its positive balancing element. Thus Dada, which was pure solvent laughter, transformed itself through reflection upon itself into the clumsy dogmatism of Surrealism. Twenty-five centuries of philosophy have left us familiar with those unforeseen turnabouts in which everything is saved when all seemed lost. Yet M. Bataille doesn't wish to save himself. Here, we might say, it is almost a question of taste: 'What characterizes man . . . ,' he writes, 'is not only the will to sufficiency, but the cunning, timid attraction toward insufficiency.'[67] This may perhaps be true of mankind; it is certainly true of M. Bataille. How are we to explain this taste for abjection which makes him write, 'I take pleasure today in being the object of disgust for the sole being to whom destiny links my life,' a sentiment in which his sensitive pride is thoroughly steeped? Is it perhaps the remnant of a long period of Christian humility? At all events, this duly elaborated inclination has become a method: how could we believe that, after ten years of Surrealist sorcery, our author could quite simply plan to achieve salvation?

> Salvation is the summit of any possible project and the pinnacle where projects are concerned . . . At the extreme limit, the desire for salvation turns into the hatred of any project (of putting off existence until later), and of salvation itself,

---

67 Bataille, *Inner Experience*, p. 88 (translation modified).

suspected of having a mundane motive . . .
salvation *was* the sole means of dissociating
eroticism . . . from the nostalgia for existing
without delay.[68]

With M. Bataille, we remain entirely in the realm
of black magic. If he quotes the famous maxim, 'whosoever would save his life shall lose it, but whosoever would
lose his life . . . shall save it,' he does so only to reject it
with all his might. The point is, indeed, to lose oneself.
But 'to lose oneself in this case would be to lose oneself
and *in no way to save oneself.*'[69] This taste for perdition
is utterly *outmoded*: we need only think back to the host
of experiences the young people of 1925 engaged in:
drugs, eroticism and all the lives lived on the toss of a
coin out of a hatred for 'making plans'. But Nietzschean
intoxication now comes and puts its stamp on this gloomy
determination. M. Bataille sees this useless, painful
sacrifice of self as the extreme of generosity: it is freely
given. And precisely because of its gratuitousness, it cannot be done coolly; it makes its appearance at the end
of Bacchic revels. Sociology can, once again, provide his
imagery: what one glimpses beneath the icy exhortations
of this solitary is nostalgia for one of those primitive
festivals in which an entire tribe becomes inebriated,
laughs, dances and copulates randomly; for one of those
festivals that are both consumption and consumation,

---

68 Bataille, *Inner Experience*, p. 47 (translation modified).

69 Bataille, *Inner Experience*, p. 22.

in which everyone, in wild, joyous frenzy, engages in self-mutilation, gaily destroys a whole year's worth of patiently amassed wealth and ends in self-destruction, going to their death singing, with neither God nor hope, carried by wine and shouting and rutting to the extremes of generosity, killing themselves *for nothing*. Hence a rejection of *askesis*. Asceticism would, in fact, put a mutilated man on the pyre. But for the sacrifice to be entire, it would have to consume man in his totality, with his laughter, passions and sexual excesses: 'If ascesis is a sacrifice, it is the sacrifice of only a part of oneself which one loses with the intention of saving the other part. But should one desire to lose oneself completely, one can do so from a movement of drunken revelry, but in no way without emotion.'[70]

Here, then, is the invitation to lose ourselves without calculation, without *quid pro quo*, without salvation. Is it sincere? We spoke not so long ago of a turnabout. It seems to me that M. Bataille has masked his own turnabout, but he has not, for all that, eliminated it. For, in the end, this loss of self is, above all, *experience*. It is 'the questioning (testing), in fever and anguish, of what man knows of the fact of being'.[71] As a result, it realizes that existence without delay that we were seeking in vain. The *ipse* is drowned in it, no doubt, but another 'oneself' arises in its stead: 'Oneself is not the subject isolating

---

70 Bataille, *Inner Experience*, p. 23 (translation modified).
71 Bataille, *Inner Experience*, p. 4 (translation modified).

itself from the world, but a place of communication, of fusion of the subject and the object.'[72] And from this conversion M. Bataille promises us marvels:

> I am and you are, in the vast flow of things, only a stopping-point favourable to resurgence. Do not delay in acquiring an exact awareness of this anguishing position. If it happened that you attached yourself to goals confined to limits in which no one was at stake but you, your life would be that of the great majority; it would be shorn of 'the marvellous'. A brief moment's halt and the complex, gentle, violent movement of worlds will make a splashing foam of your death. The glories, the marvels of your life are due to this resurgence of the wave that formed within you, to the immense cataract-like sound of the sky.[73]

And then anguish becomes frenzy, excruciating joy. Isn't this worth risking the journey for? Especially as one returns from it. For, in the end, M. Bataille writes; he has a job at the Bibliothèque Nationale; he reads, makes love and eats. As he says, in a phrase that he surely could-n't blame me for laughing at, 'I crucify myself when the fancy takes me.'[74] Why not? And we are so *won over* to this little exercise that M. Bataille calls it, 'the distance

72 Bataille, *Inner Experience*, p. 9.

73 Bataille, *Inner Experience*, p. 95 (translation amended).

74 Bataille, *Inner Experience*, p. 55 (translation amended).

man has covered in search of himself, of his glory'. He calls those who haven't been to the extremes of the possible, servants or enemies of man, not men. And suddenly this unnameable destitution takes on shape: we thought we were irredeemably lost and we were, quite simply, thereby realizing our essence: we were becoming what we are. And, at the very end of our author's explanations, we glimpse a quite different way of losing ourselves irredeemably—namely, to remain willingly within the world of the project. In that world, man flees himself and loses himself on a daily basis. He hopes for nothing and he will receive nothing. But the auto-da-fé M. Bataille offers us has all the characteristics of an apotheosis.

However, let us look at this more closely. It is, we are told, a *death agony*. We have arrived at this agony through laughter, but we could have got to it by other methods. In particular, by systematic diligence in feeling our abjection. The key thing is that we should, from the outset, *experience* this fundamental truth: being is nowhere; we are not everything, there is no everything. As a result, we can no longer 'desire to be everything'.[75] And yet 'man cannot, by any means, escape insufficiency, nor renounce ambition . . . There is no concurrence imaginable, and man, inevitably, must wish to be everything.'[76] There is no contradiction. Or, rather, this new contradiction is in the subject: we are dying from wishing for what we

---

75 Bataille, *Inner Experience*, p. x.

76 Bataille, *Inner Experience*, p. 91.

cannot give up wishing for. But this death agony is a passion: we have the duty to agonize, to raise up the whole of Nature with us to the point of agony. For it is through us that the world exists, through us, who are merely a delusion and whose ipseity is illusory. If we disappear, the world will fall back into darkness. And here we are, a flickering flame, always on the point of extinction; and the world flickers with us, it vacillates with our light. We take it in our hands and raise it to the heavens as an offering for the heavens to mark it with their seal. But the heavens are empty. Then man understands the sense of his mission. He is the One called on by all things to ask heaven for an answer that heaven refuses. 'Completed "being", from rupture to rupture, after a growing nausea had delivered it to the emptiness of the heavens, has become no longer "being", but wound, and even "agony" of all that is.'[77] And this gaping wound, which opens in the earth, beneath the endless desert of the sky, is simultaneously supplication and challenge. It is a supplication and an imploring questioning, for it seeks in vain for the All that would give it its meaning, but which hides itself. It is challenge since it knows that the All conceals itself, that it alone is responsible for the inert world, that it alone can invent its own sense and the meaning of the universe. This aspect of M. Bataille's thinking is very deeply Nietzschean. He himself uses a 'fragment' written by Nietzsche in 1880 to designate his

---

77 Bataille, *Inner Experience*, p. 80 (translation modified).

'Experience' more precisely: 'But where do those waves of everything which is great and sublime in man finally flow out? Isn't there an ocean for these torrents?—Be this ocean: there will be one,' wrote Nietzsche. And M. Bataille adds: 'the being lost of this ocean and this bare requirement: "be that ocean", designate experience and the extreme limit to which it leads'.[78] Man, an absurd creature, protesting against creation, a martyr to absurdity but re-creating himself by giving himself a meaning of his own beyond the absurd, man defiant, laughing man, Dionysian man—here, it seems to me, are the foundations of a humanism common to Nietzsche and our author.

But, thinking about it, we are not so sure of ourselves any more. M. Bataille's thought is changeable. Is he going to be content with this human, all-too-human heroism? First, let us note that he cannot properly hold to this dionysian passion he proposes; as the reader may already have noticed, by the terms of the long argument that precedes it, that passion is a swindle, a more subtle way of identifying oneself with the all, the 'everything'. Didn't M. Bataille write, in a passage we quoted above, 'Man (at the end of his quest) is . . . agony of *all that is*,' and does he not prescribe for us, in the chapter devoted to Nietzsche, 'a sacrifice in which everything is victim'?[79] At the bottom of all this, we find the old initial postulate

78 Bataille, *Inner Experience*, p. 27.

79 Bataille, *Inner Experience*, p. 130.

of dolorism, formulated by Schopenhauer and taken over by Nietzsche, that the man who suffers takes up and founds within himself the pain and evil of the universe. This is what Dionysianism or the gratuituous affirmation of the metaphysical value of suffering amounts to. There are many excuses for such an affirmation: a little distraction is permitted when one is in pain, and the idea of taking on universal suffering may serve as a balm if one manages to convince oneself of this at the appropriate point. But M. Bataille wants to be sure. He has, then, to acknowledge his bad faith: If I suffer for *everything*, I am everything, at least where suffering is concerned. If my death throes (*agonie*) are the death throes of the world, I am the world in its death throes. In this way, I shall, by losing myself, have gained *everything*.

Moreover, M. Bataille doesn't linger in this safe haven. Yet, if he leaves it, it is not for the reasons we have just stated. He does so because he wants more. The savour of Nietzschean thought derives from the fact that it is profoundly and solely earthly. Nietzsche is an atheist who harshly and logically draws all the consequences from his atheism. But M. Bataille is a shame-faced Christian. He has thrown himself into what he calls a cul-de-sac. His back is to the wall. He sums up the situation himself: 'The sky is empty . . . The ground will giveway beneath my feet. I will die in hideous conditions . . . I solicit everything negative that a laughing man can experience.'[80] And yet this hard-pressed,

---

80 Bataille, *Inner Experience*, p. 79.

cornered man will not make the admission we await from him: he will not acknowledge that *there is no* transcendence. He will prefer to play on the words, 'there is no' and 'transcendence'. We have him here and his only thought is of escape. In spite of everything, he remains what Nietzsche called, one of the 'Afterworldsmen' [*Hinterweltler*].[81] With this, the work he sets before us assumes its true meaning: the Nietzschean humanism was merely a stopping-point on his way. The true reversal comes a little later. We believed it was a question of finding man amid his wretchedness. But no, it was in fact God we had to find. Once we are aware of this, all the sophisms we have identified can be seen in a new light: they didn't arise inadvertently in some way or from precipitate judgements; they had their role to play; it was for them to persuade M. Bataille that a new kind of mysticism is possible. They were to lead us by the hand to mystical experience. It is this experience we are now going to contemplate.

III

Mysticism is *ek-stasis* or, in other words, a wresting from oneself towards, and intuitive enjoyment, of the transcendent. How can a thinker who has just asserted the absence of any transcendence achieve, in and by that very move, a mystical experience? This is the question our author has to face. Let us see how he answers it.

---

81 See Friedrich Nietzsche, *Thus Spoke Zarathustra* (R. J. Hollingdale trans.) (London: Penguin, 1961), p. 58.

Jaspers showed him the way. Has M. Bataille read the three volumes of *Philosophy*?[82] I am assured that he has not. But he is probably aware of the commentary Jean Wahl has made of it in the *Études kierkegaardiennes*. The similarities of thought and vocabulary are disquieting. For Jaspers, as for M. Bataille, the key thing is the absolute, irremediable failure of any human enterprise, which shows existence to be a 'thinking unintelligibility'. On that basis, one must 'make the leap where thought ceases'. It is the 'choice of non-knowledge' into which knowledge throws itself and in which it loses itself. For him, too, the abandonment of non-knowledge is passionate sacrifice to the world of darkness. '*Non-savoir*', '*déchirure*', '*monde de la nuit*' and '*extrême de la possibilité*'—all these expressions are common to Wahl translating Jaspers and to M. Bataille.

Our author does, however, diverge from Jaspers on one essential point. I said just now that he was in search of God. But he wouldn't agree on this. 'Mockery! that one should call me pantheist, atheist, theist! But I cry out to the sky, "I know nothing".'[83] God is still a word, a notion that helps you to leave knowledge behind, but that remains knowledge: 'God, final word meaning that all words will fail further on.'[84] M. Bataille starts out from a meditation on failure, as does Jaspers: 'Lost and

---

82 Karl Jaspers, *Philosophy* (Chicago: University of Chicago Press, 1969–71).

83 Bataille, *Inner Experience*, p. 37.

84 Bataille, *Inner Experience*, p. 36.

pleading, blind, half-dead. Like Job on the dung-heap, in the darkness of night, but imagining nothing—defenceless, knowing that all is lost.'[85] Like Jaspers, he comes to know himself as thinking unintelligibility. But as soon as he has shrouded himself in non-knowledge, he refuses any concept enabling him to designate and classify what he then attains to: 'If I said decisively: "I have seen God", that which I see would change. Instead of the inconceivable unknown—wildly free before me, leaving me wild and free before it—there would be a dead object and matter for the theologian.'[86]

Yet not everything is so clear. He now writes: 'I have of the divine an experience so mad that one will laugh at me if I speak of it' and, further on, 'God speaks to me, the idiot, face to face . . .'[87] Lastly, at the beginning of a curious chapter that contains a whole theology,[88] he again explains his refusal to name God, but in a rather different way: 'What, at bottom, deprives man of all possibility of speaking of God, is that, in human thought, God necessarily conforms to man insofar as man is weary, famished for sleep and for peace.'[89] These are no longer the scruples of an agnostic who, faced with atheism and faith, intends to keep matters in suspense. This

---

85 Bataille, *Inner Experience*, p. 35.

86 Bataille, *Inner Experience*, p. 4 (translation modified).

87 Bataille, *Inner Experience*, p. 33, p. 36.

88 Bataille, *Inner Experience*, Part Four, pp. 99–157. [Trans.]

89 Bataille, *Inner Experience*, pp. 102–03 (translation modified).

is genuinely a mystic speaking, a mystic who has seen God and rejects the all-too-human language of those who have not. The distance separating these two passages contains the whole of M. Bataille's bad faith. What has happened?

We had left our author in a cul-de-sac, with his back to the wall. In a state of atrocious, unavoidable disgust. And yet, 'man's "possible" cannot be confined to this constant disgust at himself, this dying man's rejected denial.'[90] It *cannot* be—and yet there is nothing else. The heavens are empty and man knows nothing. This is the situation M. Bataille rightly terms 'torment' and that is, if not the torment of human beings in general, at least his individual torment, his initial situation. There is no need, then, to go looking very far. This is the primary fact: M. Bataille disgusts himself. A fact considerably more terrifying in its simplicity than two hundred pages of loaded considerations on human wretchedness. Through it, I glimpse the man and his solitude. At present I know I can do nothing for him and he won't be able to do anything for me. He looks like a madman to me and I know, too, that he regards me as a madman. It is what he *is* that draws me on to the path of horror, not what he says.

But he has necessarily to fight back. Against himself. Has he not said as much? The torment he cannot escape is a torment he cannot bear either. Yet there is *nothing*

---

90 Bataille, *Inner Experience*, p. 34 (translation amended).

but that torment. So it is this very torment that is going
be doctored. The author admits this himself: 'I teach the
art of turning anguish to delight.'[91] And here is where
the slippage comes: I know nothing. Alright. That means
my knowledge goes so far and no further. Beyond that
nothing exists, since nothing is for me only what I know.
But what if I substantify my ignorance? What if I trans-
form it into the 'night of non-knowledge'? Then it
becomes something positive: I can touch it, meld myself
with it. 'With non-knowledge attained, then absolute
knowledge is simply one knowledge among others.'[92]
Better, I can settle into it. There was a light that lit up
the darkness weakly. Now, I have withdrawn into the
darkness and I look on the light *from the standpoint of
darkness*:

> Non-knowledge lays bare. This proposition is
> the summit, but must be understood in this
> way: lays bare, therefore I see what knowledge
> was hiding up to that point, but if I see, I *know*.
> Indeed, I know, but non-knowledge again lays
> bare what I have known. If nonsense is sense,
> the sense which is nonsense is lost, becomes
> nonsense again (without possible end).[93]

Our author is not to be caught so easily. If he sub-
stantifies non-knowledge, he nonetheless does so with

---

91 Bataille, *Inner Experience*, p. 35.

92 Bataille, *Inner Experience*, p. 55 (translation modified).

93 Bataille, *Inner Experience*, p. 52.

caution, as a movement, not as a thing. Nonetheless, he has pulled off the trick: non-knowledge, which previously was *nothing*, becomes the 'beyond' of knowledge. By throwing himself into it, M. Bataille suddenly finds himself *in the realm of the transcendent*. He has broken clear: the disgust, shame and nausea are left behind with knowledge. After that, little matter that he tells us 'Nothing, neither in the fall nor in the void, is revealed,'[94] for the essential thing is revealed: that my abjection is a nonsense and there is a nonsense of this nonsense (which is not, in any way, a return to the original sense). A passage from M. Blanchot cited by M. Bataille[95] shows us the trick: 'The night soon appeared to him to be darker, more terrible than any other night whatsoever, as it had really emerged from a wound of thought which could no longer think itself, *of thought captured ironically as object by something other than thought.*'[96]

But M. Bataille precisely will not see that non-knowledge is immanent to thought. A thinking that thinks it doesn't know is still thinking. It discovers its limits *from the inside*. Yet this doesn't mean it has an overview of itself. You might as well say that *nothing* has become something on the grounds that one has given it a name.

---

94 Bataille, *Inner Experience*, p. 52.

95 Albert Camus pointed out to me that *Inner Experience* is the exact translation of, and commentary on, Maurice Blanchot's *Thomas l'Obscur* (*Thomas the Obscure*, 1941).

96 From Blanchot, *Thomas the Obscure*. Cited in Bataille, *Inner Experience*, p. 101 (translation modified; Sartre's italics [Trans.]).

Indeed our author does go that far. It isn't hard to do so. You and I just write, quite straightforwardly, 'I know nothing.' But let us suppose I put inverted commas around this *nothing*. Suppose that I write, like M. Bataille, 'And, above all, "nothing", I know "nothing".' This is a *nothing* that takes on a strange form; it detaches itself, isolates itself—it is not far from existing on its own. We have only now to call it the *unknown* and our goal is achieved. The nothing is what doesn't exist at all; the unknown is what in no way exists for me. By calling the nothing the unknown, I make it the entity whose essence it is to elude the grasp of my knowledge; and if I add that I know nothing, this means that I communicate with that entity by some means other than knowledge. Here again, M. Blanchot's text, to which our author refers, brings enlightenment:

> Through this void, therefore, it was his gaze and the object of his gaze which became mingled. Not only did this eye *that saw nothing* apprehend something, but it apprehended the cause of his vision. *It saw as an object that which caused him not to see.*[97]

Here, then, is this unknown, wild and free, to which M. Bataille at times gives—and at times refuses—the name of God. It is a pure hypostatized nothingness. One last effort and we shall ourselves dissolve into the night

---

97 Blanchot, *Thomas the Obscure*. Cited in Bataille, *Inner Experience*, p. 101 (translation extensively modified).

that previously only protected us: it is knowledge that creates the *object* over against the subject. Non-knowledge is 'suppression of the object and of the subject: the only means of not resulting in the possession of the object by the subject'.[98] There remains 'communication' or, in other words, the absorbtion of everything by the night. M. Bataille forgets that he has, by his own hand, constructed a universal object: Night. And this is the moment to apply to our author what Hegel said of Schelling's absolute: 'It is the night in which all cows are black.' It would seem that this abandonment to the night is a source of delight: that comes as no surprise. It is, in fact, one particular way of dissolving oneself into the *nothing*. But that nothing is skilfully contrived in such a way that it becomes *everything*. M. Bataille, as in the case of his Nietzschean humanism above, is here satisfying in a roundabout way his desire to 'be everything'. With the words 'nothing', 'night/darkness', 'non-knowledge that lays bare', he has quite simply prepared a nice little pantheistic ecstasy for us. We remember what Poincaré said of Riemannian geometry: replace the definition of the Riemannian plane by the definition of the Euclidian sphere and you have Euclid's geometry. Similarly, just replace M. Bataille's absolute nothing by the absolute being of substance and you have Spinoza's pantheism. We must concede, of course, that Riemann's geometry isn't Euclid's. In the same way, Spinoza's system is a white and M. Bataille's a black pantheism.

---

98 Blanchot, *Thomas the Obscure*. Cited in Bataille, *Inner Experience*, p. 53.

We can, as a result, understand the function of scientism in our author's thinking. True inner experience is, in fact, poles apart from pantheism. When one has found oneself through the *cogito*, there is no longer any question of losing oneself: farewell to the abyss and the night, man takes himself with him everywhere. Wherever he is, he casts light and sees only what he casts light on; it is he who decides the meaning of things. And if somewhere he apprehends an absurd being, even if that absurd being is himself, that absurdity is still a human signification and it is he who decides on it. Man is immanent to the human; man's universe is finite, but not limited. If God speaks, he is made in the image of man. But if he remains silent, he is still human. And if there is a 'torment' for man, it is not being able to stand outside the human to judge himself, not being able to read the underside of the cards. Not because they are hidden from him, but because even if he could see them, he would be able to judge them only by his own lights. From this point of view, mystical experience must be considered as one human experience among others; it enjoys no privilege. Those who find this torment of immanence unbearable devise ruses by which to see themselves with inhuman eyes. We have seen M. Blanchot resorting to the fantastic to present us with an inhuman image of humanity. With similar motivations, M. Bataille wants to get at the human without human beings, in much the same way as Loti described 'India without the English'.[99] If he

---

99 Pierre Loti (1850–1923): a naval officer from Rochefort (Charente-Maritime) who became one of France's leading novelists. He first published *L'Inde* (*sans les Anglais*) in 1903. It has recently (2008)

manages to do this, then the game he is playing is already more than half won: he is already outside himself, has already situated himself in the realm of the transcendent. But—differing in this respect from the author of *Aminadab*—he doesn't resort to literary methods, but to the scientific attitude.

We remember Durkheim's famous precept that we should 'treat social facts as things.' This is what tempts M. Bataille in Sociology. If only he could treat social facts and human beings and himself as things, if his inexpiable individuality could only appear to him as a certain given quality, then he would be rid of himself. Unfortunately for our author, Durkheim's Sociology is dead: social facts are not things; they have meanings and, as such, they refer back to the being through whom meanings come into the world, to man, who cannot be both scientist and object of science at the same time. You might just as well try to lift the chair you are sitting on by grabbing it by its crossbars. Yet M. Bataille revels in this vain effort. It is not by chance that the word 'impossibility' flows frequently from his pen. He belongs, without a doubt, to that spiritual family whose members are susceptible, above all, to the acid, exhausting charm of impossible endeavours. It would be more appropriate to symbolize his mysticism, rather than M. Camus's humanism, by the myth of Sisyphus.

been republished by Phébus of Paris in the 'Libretto' Collection. [Trans.]

What remains of such an undertaking? First, an unde-
niable experience. I don't doubt that our author is familiar with certain ineffable states of anguish and torturous
joy. I merely note that he fails in his attempt to impart
to us the method that would enable us to obtain them
in our turn. Moreover, although his avowed ambition
was to write a mystical *Discourse on Method*, he confesses
several times that these states come and go as and when
it suits them. For my part, I see them, rather, as defensive
reactions specific to M. Bataille, appropriate to his case
alone. In the way that hunted animals sometimes react
with what is known as 'the fake death reflex', the supreme
escapism, our author, pinned to the rear wall of his cul-
de-sac, escapes his disgust by a sort of ecstatic fainting fit.
But even if he were able to make available to us a rigorous
method for obtaining these delights at will, we would be
within our rights to ask: what of it? Inner experience, we
are told, is the opposite of the 'project'. But we *are*
projects, despite what our author says. And we are not so
out of cowardice or to flee from anxiety: we are projects
from the first. If such a state is to be pursued, then, it is
to be sought as a basis for new projects. Christian mysticism is a project: it is eternal life that is at issue. But, if
the joys to which M. Bataille invites us are to be purely
self-referential, if they are not to be part of the fabric of
new undertakings and contribute to shaping a new
humanity that will surpass itself towards new goals, then
they are of no greater value than the pleasure of drinking
a glass of brandy or of sunning oneself on a beach.

Rather than with this unusable experience, then, we shall concern ourselves more with the man who reveals himself in these pages, with his 'sumptuous, bitter' soul, his pathological pride, his self-disgust, his eroticism, his often magnificent eloquence, his rigorous logic that masks the incoherence of his thought, his passion-induced bad faith and his fruitless quest for impossible escape. But literary criticism runs up against its limits here. The rest is a matter for psychoanalysis. Yet before anyone protests, I do not have in mind the crude, questionable methods of Freud, Adler or Jung; there are other schools of psychoanalysis.

December 1943

AMINADAB,
OR THE FANTASTIC CONSIDERED
AS A LANGUAGE

Thought taken ironically for an object
by something other than thought.

Maurice Blanchot, *Thomas l'Obscur* [1]

Thomas is moving through a small town. Who is Thomas?
Where is he from? Where is he going? We shall have no
answers to these questions. A woman beckons to him
from a house. He goes in and suddenly finds himself in
a strange community of tenants, in which everyone seems
both to lay down the law and to be subject to it. He is
made to undergo some incoherent initiation rites; he is
chained to an almost speechless companion and wanders,
still yoked to that companion, from room to room

---

1 Maurice Blanchot, *Thomas the Obscure* (Robert Lamberton trans.)
(New York: Hill Press, 1988), p. 14.

and floor to floor, often forgetting what he is looking for, but remembering always just in time when they try to detain him. After many adventures, he changes, loses his companion and falls ill. It is at this point that he receives his last warnings. An old employee tells him, 'The person you should be interrogating is yourself,'[2] and a nurse adds, 'you have been the victim of an illusion; you thought someone was calling you, but no one was there, and the call came from you.'[3] He persists nonetheless, gets to the upper floors and finds the woman who had waved to him. But he does so only to be told, 'No order called you here, and someone else was expected.'[4] Thomas has gradually weakened. At nightfall, the companion to whom he was earlier chained comes back to see him and explains that Thomas has taken a wrong turning.

> You didn't recognize your own way . . . I was like another you. I knew all the pathways of the house, and I knew which one you ought to have followed. All you had to do was ask me.[5]

Thomas asks a last question, but it remains unanswered and the room is flooded with the darkness from

---

2 Maurice Blanchot, *Aminadab* (Jeff Fort trans.) (Lincoln and London: University of Nebraska Press, 2002), p. 123.

3 Blanchot, *Aminadab,* p. 154.

4 Blanchot, *Aminadab,* p. 192.

5 Blanchot, *Aminadab,* p. 184.

outside, 'beautiful and soothing . . . a vast dream which is not within the reach of the person it envelops'.[6] Summarized like this, M. Blanchot's intentions seem very clear. What is even clearer is the extraordinary resemblance of his book to the novels of Kafka. The same meticulous, urbane style, the same nightmarish civility, the same weird, starchy ceremoniousness, the same pointless quests—pointless since they lead to nothing; the same exhaustive, stagnant reasoning; and the same sterile initiations—sterile because they are not initiations into anything. M. Blanchot states that he had read nothing of Kafka's when he wrote *Aminadab*. This leaves us even greater scope to marvel at the strange encounter that led this young and as yet uncertain writer to rediscover, in his quest to express some banal ideas on human life, the instrument that once produced such unprecedented sounds in other hands.

I don't know how this conjunction came about. It interests me only because it enables me to draw up the 'latest balance sheet' of the literature of the fantastic. For fantasy, like the other literary genres, has an essence and a history, the latter being merely the development of the former. What, then, must the nature of the contemporary fantastic genre be if a French writer—and, moreover, one convinced of the need to 'think French'[7]—is

6 Blanchot, *Aminadab*, p. 196.

7 M. Blanchot was, I believe, a disciple of Charles Maurras. [J.-P. S.] On Maurras, see NOTE 6, p. 181. [Trans.]

able to find himself at one with a writer from Central Europe as soon as he adopts this mode of expression?

To achieve the fantastic, it is neither necessary nor sufficient to depict the extraordinary. If it occurs singly in a law-governed world, then the oddest event will become part of the order of the universe. If you make a horse talk, then I shall believe it is momentarily bewitched. But if it goes on talking amid trees that don't move and on ground that remains where it is, I shall grant him the natural power of speech. I shall no longer see the horse, but the man in the horse costume. If, on the other hand, you manage to persuade me that this horse is fantastical, then the trees, earth and rivers are so too, even if you haven't mentioned the fact. One doesn't make occasional allowances for the fantastical; either it doesn't exist or it extends to the whole of the universe; it is a complete world in which things manifest a captive, tormented form of thinking, both whimsical and connected, that gnaws away from below at the linkages of the mechanism, without their ever managing to express themselves. In that world, matter is never wholly matter, since it offers only the perpetually thwarted rudiments of determinism, and mind is never wholly mind, since it has sunk into slavery and been impregnated and coarsened by matter. All is woe: things suffer and tend towards inertia, without ever quite achieving it; the humiliated, enslaved mind strives unsuccessfully after consciousness and freedom. The fantastic offers an inverse image of the union of soul and body: the soul takes the place of the body and the body that of the soul. And we cannot form clear, distinct ideas with which to think this image; we have to resort to confused thoughts that are themselves fantastical; in short, though we are wide-awake, fully mature and entirely civilized, we have to give in to the 'magical' mentality of the dreamer, the child and the primitive. There is no need, then, to resort to fairies; in themselves, fairies are simply pretty women; what is fantastical is nature when it bends to the fairies' will; this is nature outside of man or within man, when man is conceived as a creature turned upside down.

So long as we thought it possible to escape the human condition by asceticism, mysticism, the metaphysical disciplines or the practice of poetry, the genre of fantasy had a clearly defined role to fulfil. It manifested our human power to transcend the human. We strove to create a world that was not this world, either because, like Poe, we preferred artifice in principle, because we believed, with Cazotte,[8] Rimbaud and all those who strove to see 'a drawing-room at the bottom of a lake'[9] that the writer had a magical mission, or, alternatively, because, like Lewis Carroll, we wanted to apply systematically to literature that unconditional power the mathematician has of engendering a universe from a

---

8 Jacques Cazotte (1719–92): a French author of fantastical tales and romances. [Trans.]

9 Arthur Rimbaud, *A Season in Hell* (Oliver Bernard trans.) (London: Penguin, 1995), p. 37.

small number of conventions or, lastly, because, like Nodier,[10] we had recognized that the writer is, first, a liar and we wanted to achieve the absolute lie. The object thus created was entirely self-referential; its aim was not to depict, but only to exist; it compelled acceptance through its own density alone. If certain authors happened to take over the language of the fantasy genre to express some philosophical or moral ideas under cover of agreeable fictions, they willingly acknowledged that they had diverted this mode of expression from its usual ends and had merely created, so to speak, a *trompe-l'oeil* form of the fantastic.

M. Blanchot is beginning to write in a period of disillusionment. After the great metaphysical carnival of the post-war years, which ended in disaster, the writers and artists of the new generation have, out of pride, humility and seriousness, made a widely-trumpeted return to the human. This trend has had an impact on the fantastic itself. For Kafka, who figures as a forerunner here, there was no doubt a transcendent reality, but it is out of reach and serves only to make us feel man's abandonment within the realm of the human the more cruelly. M. Blanchot, who doesn't believe in transcendence, would no doubt subscribe to the following opinion expressed by Eddington: 'We have found a strange footprint on the shores of the unknown. We have devised profound

---

10 Charles Nodier (1780–1844): a French novelist and author of fantastical tales. [Trans.]

theories, one after another, to account for its origins. At last, we have succeeded in reconstructing the creature that made the footprint. And lo! It is our own.'[11] Hence the tentative moves towards a 'return to the human' on the part of the literature of fantasy. Admittedly, it will not be used to prove anything or to enlighten. M. Blanchot, in particular, denies that he has written one of those allegories whose 'meaning', as he puts it, 'corresponds unequivocally to the story, but can also be explained entirely apart from it'. It is simply the case that, to take its place within contemporary humanism, the fantastic is domesticating itself like the other genres, giving up on the exploration of transcendent realities, and resigning itself to transcribing the human condition. And at around this same moment, as a result of internal factors, this literary genre has been pursuing its own line of development and getting rid of fairies, genies and hob-goblins as useless, time-worn conventions. Dali and de Chirico showed us a nature that was haunted, but freed, nonetheless, from the supernatural: the one depicted the life and sufferings of stones, while the other illustrated an accursed biology, showing us the horrible sprouting of human bodies or of metals contaminated with life. By a curious twist, the new humanism further hastens this development: M. Blanchot, following Kafka, is no longer concerned to recount the bewitchings of matter; Dali's monsters of meat probably seemed like clichés to

---

11 The quotation is from Sir Arthus Eddington's *Space, Time and Gravitation* (Cambridge: Cambridge University Press, 1920). [Trans.]

him, as haunted castles had to Dali. For him, only one fantastical object remains: man. Not the man of religion and spiritualism, who is only half-committed to the things of this world, but given man, natural man, social man—the man who acknowledges a hearse as it passes, who shaves by a window, who kneels in churches, who marches behind a flag. That being is a microcosm. He is the world, the whole of nature: in him alone can the whole of spellbound   nature be revealed. In him. Not in his body—M. Blanchot renounces physiological fantasies; his characters are physically undistinguished; he describes them with a single word, in passing—but in his total reality as *homo faber, homo sapiens.* And so the fantastic, in humanizing itself, comes closer to the ideal purity of its essence and becomes what it was. It has rid itself, it seems, of all its trickery. There is nothing up its sleeve now and we recognize that the footprint on the shore is our own. No succubi, no ghosts, no weeping fountains—there are only human beings and the fantasy creator announces that he identifies with the fantasy object. For contemporary man, the fantastic is now just one way among a hundred others of reflecting back his own image.

It is on the basis of these remarks that we can try to gain a better understanding of the extraordinary resemblance between *Aminadab* and Kafka's *Castle.* We have seen that the essence of the fantastic is to offer an inverted image of the union between soul and body. Now, we have seen that in both Kafka and Blanchot, the fantastic confines itself to expressing the human world. Is it not going to find itself subject, in the work of both authors, to new conditions? And what can the inversion of human relations mean here?

When I come into a café, the first things I see are implements. Not things, not raw materials, but utensils, tables, benches, mirrors, glasses and saucers. Each of them represents a piece of subjugated matter. Taken together, they are part of a manifest order. And the meaning of their ordering is a purpose, an end—an end that is myself or, rather, the man in me, the consumer that I am. This is what the human world is like, when it is *the right way up.* We would look in vain for a 'raw' material: the means functions here as the matter, and the form—the spiritual order—is represented by the end or purpose. Let us now depict this café *turned upside down.* We shall have to show ends that are crushed by their very own means, which are attempting unsuccessfully to burst through enormous thicknesses of matter; or, alternatively, objects which of themselves show their instrumentality, but do so with a force of indiscipline and disorder, a kind of woolly independence that causes their purpose to elude us just when we think we have grasped it. Here is a door, for example: it is there with its hinges, handle and lock. It is carefully bolted, as though protecting some treasure or other. After trying various different approaches, I manage to procure the key: I unlock it and find that it opens on to a wall. I sit down and order a coffee. The waiter has me repeat the order three times and repeats it himself to eliminate all possibility of error. He dashes off, passes my order on to a second waiter, who writes it in a notebook and hands it to a third. In the end, a fourth waiter comes back; 'Here you are,' he says, and places an inkwell on my table. 'But I ordered a coffee,' I say. 'That's right,' he says, as he walks off. If, when reading tales of this sort, the reader is able to think this is a practical joke being played by the waiters or some collective psychosis, then we have failed in our efforts. But if we have managed to convey the impression that we are speaking to him of a world in which these bizarre happenings represent normal behaviour, then he will be plunged at once into the heart of the fantastic. This *human* form of the fantastic is the revolt of means against ends: either the object in question noisily asserts itself as a means and, by the violence of that   assertion, conceals its own end or purpose, or it refers on to another and another in an infinite succession without our ever being able to discover any supreme end or, by some confusion of means that really belong to unrelated series, we are left with a glimpse of a scrambled, composite image of contradictory ends.

Let us imagine, on the other hand, that I have managed to perceive an end. In that case, I find all my bridges are burned. I cannot discover or devise any means to achieve it. I have an appointment with someone on the first floor of this café; I have to get up there urgently. I can see this first floor from down below. Its balcony is visible from a large circular opening. I can even see tables and customers at those tables. But though I walk a hundred times round the room I cannot find a stairway. In this case, the means is precisely specified; everything points to and calls for it; it is latent in the manifest presence of the end. But things have reached such an extreme that it simply doesn't exist. Is this to be described as an 'absurd' world, such as M. Camus speaks of in his *Outsider*? But the absurd is a total absence of ends. The absurd can be conceived clearly and distinctly; it belongs to the world *the right way up*, as limited *de facto* by human powers. In the obsessive, hallucinatory world we are trying to describe, the absurd would be an oasis, a respite; hence there is no place for it. I cannot pause there for a moment. Every means sends me relentlessly to the ghost of an end that haunts it, and every end to the ghost of a means by which I could achieve it. I cannot form any kind of thought, except in slippery, shimmering notions that fall to pieces as I examine them.

Given all this, it is not surprising that, in authors as different as Kafka and Blanchot, we find strictly identical themes. Is it not this same preposterous world they are attempting to depict? It will be the first concern of both to exclude 'impassive nature' from their novels: hence the stifling atmosphere that is common to both. The struggle of the hero of Kafka's *Trial* takes place in a city;

he crosses streets and enters buildings. Thomas in *Aminadab* wanders around the interminable corridors of a block of flats. Neither of them ever sees forests, meadows or hills. And yet how restful it would be if they could find themselves in the presence of a mound of earth, of a fragment of matter that had *no purpose*! But, were they to do so, the fantastic would vanish in an instant. The law of the genre condemns them never to encounter anything but tools. These tools, as we have seen, are not intended to serve them, but to provide relentless evidence of a strange, elusive purpose: hence this labyrinth of corridors, doors and staircases that lead nowhere; hence these signposts indicating nothing, the countless signs that stud the roads and have no meaning. We should cite as a particular case of the theme of signs the message motif that is so important to both Kafka and Blanchot. In the right-way-up world, the existence of a message implies a sender, a messenger and a recipient. It is itself merely a means; its content is the end. In the upside-down world, the means becomes autonomous and self-contained: we are plagued by messages without content, messengers or senders. Or, alternatively, the end exists, but the means gradually gnaws away at it. In one of Kafka's tales, the emperor sends a message to one of the townspeople, but the messenger has such a long way to go that the message will never reach its destination. For his part, M. Blanchot tells us of a message whose contents change progressively in the course of its journey. He writes:

All these hypotheses . . . make the following conclusion seem most likely; namely that, despite his good will, the messenger, upon arriving upstairs, will have forgotten his message and will be unable to transmit it; or else, assuming he has scrupulously retained the terms in which it was formulated, it will be impossible for him to understand its meaning, for what has a certain meaning here must have a completely different one there, or perhaps none at all; . . . What he himself will have become, I refuse to imagine, for I assume that he will be as different from what I am as the transmitted message will be different from the one that is received.[12]

It may also happen that a message reaches us and is partially decipherable. But we learn later that it wasn't intended for us. In *Aminadab*, M. Blanchot discovers another possibility: a message comes through to me, which is, of course, incomprehensible. I enquire into it and find out, in the end, that I was the sender. Needless to say, these eventualities do not represent strokes of ill luck among other possible outcomes. They are part of the *nature* of the message. The sender knows this and the recipient isn't unaware of it; yet they go on relentlessly sending and receiving messages, as though the great thing were the message itself, not its content. But the means has absorbed the end as surely as a blotter absorbs ink.

12 Blanchot, *Aminadab*, p. 147.

For the same reason as they banish nature from their narratives, our two authors also banish natural man, that is to say, the isolated person, the individual, the one Céline calls a 'fellow of no collective importance', who can be no other than an absolute end. The fantastic imperative stands the Kantian imperative on its head. 'Act always in such a way,' it tells us, 'that you treat the human in yourself and in others as a means and never as an end.' In order to plunge their heroes into feverish, exhausting, unintelligible activity, Messrs. Blanchot and Kafka have to surround them with instrument-men. Sent from instrument to man as he might be from means to end, the reader discovers that man, in his turn, is merely a means. Hence the functionaries, soldiers and judges who people Kafka's works, and the domestics, also known as 'employees', in *Aminadab*. As a result, the fantastic universe assumes the appearance of a bureaucracy: it is, in fact, the great departments of state that most resemble a society turned upside down; Thomas in *Aminadab* goes from office to office, from clerk to clerk, without ever finding the employer or the man in charge, like those visitors petitioning a ministry who are sent endlessly from one department to another. Moreover, the acts of these functionaries remain wholly unintelligible. In the normally constituted world, I can distinguish reasonably well a magistrate's sneeze, which is an accident, or his whistling, which is a matter of whim, from his juridical activity, which is the application of the law. In the upside-down world, the meticulous, pernickety employees of the fantastical world will seem at first to be diligently carrying out their functions. But I shall soon learn that their zeal is bereft of meaning—or even reprehensible: it is mere whim. By contrast, some sudden action that outrages me by its inappropriateness turns out, on closer examination, to be entirely in keeping with the social dignity of the character concerned; it was carried out according to the law. In this way, the law collapses into whim and whim affords a sudden insight into the law. I would look in vain here for rulebooks, regulations and decrees: ancient commands lie around on desks and the employees conform to them without it being clear whether these orders have been issued by someone in authority, whether they are the product of centuries-old, anonymous routines or whether indeed they have not been invented by the functionaries themselves. Even the scope of these orders is ambiguous and I shall never be able to decide whether they apply to all members of the community or only to me. Yet this ambiguous law, which wavers between rule and whim, between the universal and the singular, is present everywhere. It holds you in its grip, overwhelms you. You transgress it when you think you are obeying and, when you think you are rebelling, you find your are obeying it unwittingly. Ignorance is no excuse and yet no one knows what the law actually is. Its aim is not to maintain order or regulate human relations. It is simply the Law, without purpose, meaning or content, and no one can escape it.

But the circle must be closed: no one can enter the world of dreams other than by sleeping; similarly, no one can enter the world of the fantastic other than by becoming fantastical themselves. Now, we know that when the reader begins reading he identifies with the hero of the novel. It is, then, the hero who, by lending us his point of view, provides the only path of access to the fantastic. The old technique presented him as a normally constituted individual transported miraculously into a world turned upside down. Kafka employed this process at least once. In *The Trial*, K. is a normal man. We can see the advantage of this technique; by creating a contrast, it throws the strange character of the new world into relief and the fantastic novel becomes an *Erziehungsroman*. The reader shares in the protagonist's amazement and follows him from discovery to discovery. Only, at the same time, he sees the fantastic *from the outside*, as a spectacle, as though a waking rational consciousness were peacefully contemplating the images of our dreams. In *The Castle*, Kafka perfected his technique. Here, the protagonist is himself a fantastic creature. We know nothing about this surveyor, whose adventures and views we are to share, other than his unintelligible determination to remain in a forbidden village. To achieve this goal, he sacrifices everything; he treats himself as a means. But we shall never know the value this goal had for him, nor whether it was worth so much effort. M. Blanchot has adopted the same method; his Thomas is no less mysterious than the domestic servants in the building. We don't know where he comes from, nor why he is so eager to get to the woman who beckoned to him. Like Kafka, like Samsa, like the Surveyor, Thomas *is never surprised*: he is, however, outraged, as though the series of events he witnesses seemed perfectly natural to him, but reprehensible, as though he had within him a strange norm of Good and Evil about which M. Blanchot has carefully omitted to inform us. So we are forced, by the very laws of the novel, to espouse a viewpoint that is not our own, to condemn without comprehending and to contemplate with no surprise things that astound us. Furthermore, M. Blanchot opens and closes his hero's soul like a box. We can at times get inside it, at others we are left outside. And when we are inside, we find lines of reasoning that have already begun, that link together in mechanical sequence and presuppose principles and purposes of which we know nothing. We fall into line, because we *are* the hero and reason with him; but these lines of thinking never come to anything, as though the reasoning alone were all that counted. Once again, the means has consumed the end. And our reason, which was about to set aright a world turned upside down, is swept up in the nightmare and becomes, itself, fantastical. M. Blanchot has gone even further than this. In an excellent passage in *Aminadab*, his hero suddenly discovers that he is, without knowing it, employed in the building and that he has the role of executioner there. We had patiently questioned the functionaries, since it seemed to us that they knew the law and the secrets of the universe, and suddenly we learn that we were ourselves functionaries and didn't know it. So now the others turn imploring gazes on us and question us in turn. Perhaps we know the law after all. 'To know,' says Alain, 'is to know that we know.' But this is a maxim from the normally con- stituted world. In the world turned upside down, we don't know that we know what we know; and when we know that we know, we don't know. In this way, our last resort, that self-consciousness in which stoicism sought refuge, eludes us and disintegrates. Its transparency is the transparency of the void; our very being is outside and in the hands of others.

These, in outline, are the central themes of *The Castle* and *Aminadab*. I hope I have shown that they are inevitable once the decision has been made to depict a world turned upside down. But, you will object, why does it have to be depicted that way? What a stupid plan, to show human beings with their legs in the air! This world is not, in fact, fantastical, for the very good reason that everything in it is the right way up. A horror novel might present itself as a mere transposition of reality, because one does meet with some horrible situations in the normal course of events. But, as we have seen, there cannot be any *fantastical* events, because the fantastic can exist only as a universe. Let us examine this more closely. If I am the wrong way up in a topsy-turvy world, then to me everything seems the right way up. If I were fantastical and inhabited a fantastical world, I could in no way regard it as such. This will help us to understand our authors' intentions.

I cannot, then, judge this world, because my judgements are part of it. If I conceive it as a work of art or as a complicated mechanism, I do so employing human notions. And if, on the other hand, I declare it absurd, I do so again by means of human concepts. As for the ends pursued by our species, how am I to describe them, except in relation to other ends? I may hope, at a pinch, to know the detail of the mechanism surrounding me one day, but how could man judge the world in its totality— that is to say, the world with man in it? It is, however, my ambition to know what really goes on; I would like to contemplate humanity as it is. The artist stubbornly persists when the philosopher has given up. He invents convenient fictions to satisfy our curiosity: Micromégas,[13] the noble savage, the dog Riquet[14] or that 'Outsider' M. Camus recently told us about—pure gazes that stand outside the human condition and are, therefore, able to inspect it. In the eyes of these angels, the human world is a *given* reality; they can say that it is this or that and

13 Micromégas is the hero of Voltaire's satirical *conte* of the same name, which was originally published in London in 1752. He is a 120,000-foot-tall inhabitant of Sirius who visits Earth in 1737. [Trans.]

14 Riquet is the dog of Monsieur Bergeret, a recurring character in the novels of Anatole France. [Trans.]

that it could be different. Human ends are contingent; they are mere facts that the angels consider, as we consider the ends of bees and ants. Human progress is a mere running on the spot, since man can no more jump out of this finite, limited world than the ant can escape from his ant's universe. Only, by forcing the reader to identify with an inhuman hero, we send him soaring above the human condition. He escapes; he loses sight of that prime necessity of the universe he is contemplating— namely, that man is inside it. How can we have him see *from outside* this obligation to be inside? Ultimately, this is the problem Blanchot and Kafka set themselves. It is an exclusively literary and technical problem, which would have no meaning at the philosophical level. And here is the solution they have found: they have eliminated the angelic perspective and have plunged the reader into the world, with K. and with Thomas. But they have left to hover within this immanence something like a ghost of transcendence. The instruments, actions and purposes are all familiar to us, and we are on such intimate terms with them that they are barely noticeable. But at the very point when we feel enveloped, with them, by a warm atmosphere of organic sympathy, they are presented to us in a cold, strange light. This brush is here in my hand. I merely have to pick it up to brush my clothes. But on the point of touching it, I stop. It is a brush seen from outside. It is there in all its contingency; it refers to contingent ends, as seems to be the case to human eyes with the white pebble the ant stupidly pulls towards its hole. 'They brush their clothes every morning,' the Angel would say. And that is all it would take for the activity to seem obsessive and unintelligible. In M. Blanchot's case, there is no angel, but the effort is made, nonetheless, to make us conceive *our* ends—those ends that arise with us and give meaning to our lives—as *ends for others*. We are shown merely the external aspect of these alienated, paralysed ends, the side that they show to the outside, the side that makes them *facts*. These are petrified ends, ends seen from their underside, invaded by materiality and registered before our will has willed them. As a consequence, the means are cast adrift again. If it is no longer clear you have to brush yourself every morning, then the brush comes to seem like an indecipherable implement, the relic of some vanished civilization. It still signifies something, like those pipe-shaped tools they found at Pompeii. But no one now knows what it signifies. What, pray, is the world of the fantastic but the combination of these immobilized ends and these monstrous, futile means? The method is clear here: since human activity, when seen from outside, seems upside down, Kafka and Blanchot, seeking to have us see our condition from the outside but without resorting to angels, have depicted a world turned upside down. A contradictory world, in which mind becomes matter, since values appear as facts, and in which matter is grawed away by mind, since everything is simultaneously both a means and an end—a world in which, while continuing to be inside it, I see myself from the outside. We can conceive this world only with evanescent, self-destroying concepts. Or, more accurately, we cannot conceive it at all. This is why M. Blanchot writes, '[The meaning] can be grasped only through a fiction and dissipates as soon as we try to understand it in itself . . . The story . . . seems mysterious, because it expresses everything that will not, in fact, bear expression.' There is a kind of marginal existence of the fantastic: look it directly in the eye, try to express its meaning in words and it vanishes, because you have to be either inside it or outside. But if you read the story without attempting to translate it, it attacks you from the sides. The few truths you fish out of *Aminadab* will become colourless and lifeless the moment they are out of the water. Yes, of course, man is alone, he decides his destiny alone, he invents the law to which he is subject; each of us, though a stranger to himself, is a victim and a tormentor for everyone else; in vain do we try to transcend the human condition; it would be better to acquire a Nietzschean sense of earthliness. Yes, of course, M. Blanchot's wisdom seems to belong among those 'transcendences' Jean Wahl referred to when speaking of Heidegger. But in the end, none of this has a particularly new ring to it. And yet when these truths were slipping upstream, through the currents of the narrative, they had a strange gleam about them. This is because we were seeing them wrong side up: they were fantastical truths.

Our authors, who had travelled such a long way together, part company at this point. Of Kafka I have nothing to say, except that he is one of the rarest, greatest writers of our time. And then he came first. In him the chosen technique met a need. If he shows us human life perpetually disturbed by an impossible transcendence, he does so because he believes in the existence of that transcendence. It is simply beyond our grasp. His universe is both fantastical and rigorously true. M. Blanchot has, admittedly, considerable talent. But he comes second and the artifices he employs are already too familiar to us. Commenting on Jean Paulhan's *Les Fleurs de Tarbes*, he has written:

> Those who, by prodigious efforts of asceticism, had the illusion of distancing themselves from all literature through the attempt to rid themselves of conventions and forms, in order to gain direct access to the secret world and profound metaphysics they wished to reveal . . . contented themselves in the end with using that world, that secret and that metaphysics as conventions and forms which they displayed with self-satisfaction and which constituted the visible armature and core of their works . . . For that kind of writer, metaphysics, religion and feelings take the place of technique and language. They are a system of expression, a literary genre—in a word, literature.[15]

15 Maurice Blanchot, *Comment la littérature est-elle possible?* (Paris: José Corti, 1942), p. 23.

I am rather afraid that this criticism, if it is a criticism, may be directed at M. Blanchot himself. The system of signs he has chosen doesn't entirely correspond to the thought he expresses. To depict for us the 'nature of the mind, its deep division, this battle of the Same with the Same, which is the means of its power, its torment and its apotheosis', there was no point resorting to artifices that introduce an external gaze into the heart of consciousness. I would happily say of M. Blanchot what Lagneau said of Barrès: 'He stole the tool.'[16] And this slight discrepancy between sign and signified relegates what in Kafka were living themes to the rank of literary conventions. Thanks to M. Blanchot, there is now a stereotype of the 'Kafkaesque' fantastic, in the same way as there is a stereotype of haunted castles and blood-spattered monsters. And I know that art lives by conventions, but they have, at least, to be properly chosen. Seen against a transcendence tinged with Maurrassianism, the fantastic looks like something that has been tacked on.

The reader's unease increases because M. Blanchot doesn't remain faithful to his original intention. He has told us that he wants the meaning of *Aminadab* to 'dissipate as soon as we seek to understand it for itself'. Well and good, but why then does he offer us a perpetual translation of its symbols and a copious commentary on

---

16 Maurice Barrès (1862–1923): a novelist, journalist and political activist; close to the Symbolist movement in his youth, he came to be associated with extreme nationalism and a current of pre-fascist romanticism in early-twentieth-century French literature. [Trans.]

them? In many places, the explanations become so insistent that the story comes to look like an allegory. Select at random any page of the long narrative in which the myth of the domestics is developed. Take the following, for example:

> I have told you that the staff is invisible most of the time. What a foolish thing to say; I gave in to a prideful temptation and am now ashamed of it. The staff invisible? Invisible most of the time? We never see them, ever, not even from a distance; we do not even know what the word *see* could mean when it comes to them, nor if there is a word to express their absence, nor even if the thought of this absence is not a supreme and pitiful resource to make us hope for their coming. The state of negligence in which they keep us is, from a certain point of view, unimaginable. We could therefore complain about how indifferent they are to our interests, since many of us have seen our health ruined or have paid with our lives for mistakes made by the service. Yet we would be prepared to forgive everything if from time to time they gave us some satisfaction . . .[17]

Take the above passage and replace the word 'staff' with the word 'God', the word 'service' with 'providence' and you will have an entirely intelligible account of a

17 Blanchot, *Aminadab*, p. 75.

certain aspect of the religious feeling. Often, too, the objects of this falsely fantastical world yield their meaning 'the right way up', without need of any commentary, such as the companion in chains that so clearly stands for the body—the body humiliated and mistreated in a society that has divorced the physical from the spiritual. At this point we seem to be translating a translation, to be translating back words that had originated in our own language.

I don't, in fact, claim to have grasped all the author's intentions and perhaps I am wrong about many of them. It was a sufficient source of unease that these intentions were obvious, even when they were obscure. It was always in my mind that, with more application or more intelligence, I would have got to the bottom of them. In Kafka, the various accidents of the narrative are connected by the needs of the plot: in *The Trial*, for example, we never for a moment lose sight of the fact that K. is fighting for his dignity and his life. But what is Thomas fighting for? He has no clear-cut character, he has no aim, he is barely of any interest. And events accumulate capriciously. As in life, one might say. But life isn't a novel, and these successions of events, with no rhyme or reason to them, that we can discern in the work itself, send us back, in spite of ourselves, to the author's secret intentions. Why does Thomas lose his partner in chains, and does he fall ill? Nothing in the world turned upside down prepares or explains this illness. Its *raison d'être* must lie outside that world, in the author's providential intentions. Most of the time, then, M. Blanchot is wasting his effort; he doesn't succeed in ensnaring his reader in the nightmarish world he is depicting. The reader escapes; he is outside, outside with the author himself. He is contemplating these dreams as he would a well-oiled machine; only at very rare moments does he lose his foothold.

As it happens, these moments are enough to show up M. Blanchot as a writer of quality. He is ingenious and subtle, sometimes profound, and he loves words. All that is missing is for him to find his style. His incursion into the realm of the fantastic is not without consequence: it makes something clear. Kafka was inimitable. He remained on the horizon as a perpetual temptation. By having imitated him unwittingly, M. Blanchot frees us from his thrall; he brings his methods out into the open. Once catalogued, classified, ossified and useless, they lose their frightening or dizzying effects. Kafka was merely a stage; through him, as through Hoffmann, Poe, Lewis Carroll and the Surrealists, the literature of the fantastic continues the steady progress that will inevitably unite it, ultimately, with what it has always been.

＊

A NOTE ON SOURCES

'A New Mystic'

Originally published as 'Un nouveau mystique' in *Situations I* (Paris: Gallimard, 1947), pp. 133–74.

First published in English translation in *Critical Essays* (London: Seagull Books, 2010), pp. 219–93.

'*Aminadab*, or the Fantastic Considered as a Language'

Originally published as '*Aminadab* ou du fantastique considéré comme un langage' in *Situations I* (Paris: Gallimard, 1947), pp. 29–32.

First published in English translation in *Critical Essays* (London: Seagull Books, 2010), pp. 185–218.